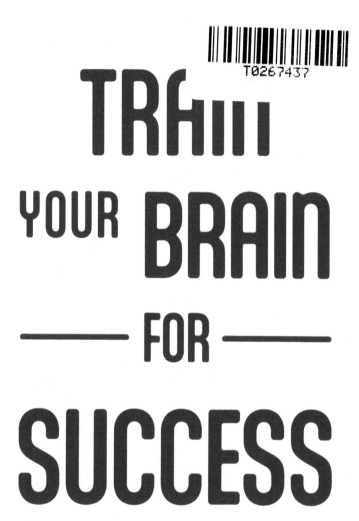

# TRAIN
## YOUR BRAIN
## — FOR —
## SUCCESS

# TRAIN YOUR BRAIN FOR —— SUCCESS

Read **Smarter,** Remember **More,** and **Break Your Own Records**

## ROGER SEIP

WILEY

Copyright © 2024 by John Wiley & Sons, Inc. All rights reserved.

Published by John Wiley & Sons, Inc., Hoboken, New Jersey.
Published simultaneously in Canada.

For general information on our other products and services or for technical support, please contact our Customer Care Department within the United States at (800) 762-2974, outside the United States at (317) 572-3993 or fax (317) 572-4002.

Wiley also publishes its books in a variety of electronic formats. Some content that appears in print may not be available in electronic formats. For more information about Wiley products, visit our web site at www.wiley.com.

*Library of Congress Cataloging-in-Publication Data is Available:*

ISBN 9781394190454 (Paperback)
ISBN 9781118330555 (ePub)
ISBN 9781118333389 (ePDF)

Cover design: Wiley

SKY10054607_090423

# Contents

# Foreword

People don't tap into their full potential.

Nearly everyone (certainly anyone who would pick up this book) wants their results to significantly improve. They want to grow, thrive, and make a huge impact, but the majority of their God-given potential isn't being used.

In the pursuit of personal development, most people make two dire mistakes. First, they look outside themselves for the answers. They believe that there's a magic bullet that someone has forged, and if they could only get their hands on that elusive magic bullet, everything would change for them.

Of course, nobody admits that they are looking for a magic bullet. Deep down inside, however, most people really hope that someday their magic bullet will magically appear.

After people resign themselves to the fact that there is no magic bullet, they commit the second mistake. They make the process of growth way more complex than it really is. In an attempt to take personal responsibility and fully engage, all but a very wise few overcomplicate the simple steps that create huge personal growth.

This brilliant book has no magic bullets. It is simple without being simplistic. What you will find are foundational skills and fundamental truths that have been around for thousands of years, yet are still missing from most people's lives. These skills are fun to learn, interesting to study, and remarkably easy to apply.

I've traveled with, lived with, and worked with Roger Seip for more than two decades. I've watched him *do* the things that he teaches here, and he's living proof that when you understand and apply the fundamentals, you win.

Although there are no magic bullets, the results certainly *seem* magical. Tripling your ability to remember information! Reading two or three or even four times faster than you do now! Crafting goals that propel you toward them, and utilizing time in a way that allows the achievement of everything that's really important!

From the outside looking in, these are impossible feats, right?

Not at all. These are simply the foundations that any committed student of this book will experience. And that is only the beginning.

The principles and stories shared in this book work. They've worked for thousands of people just like you. Your task is to be bold enough to believe that you too can do extraordinary things, teachable enough to let this powerfully simple information sink in, and then accountable enough to act on it. Be free!

—Eric Plantenberg
President of Freedom Personal Development
Creator of The Abundant Living Retreat

# Introduction
# How to Break Records

The very first motivational speaker I heard as an adult was a gentleman named Mort Utley. I experienced his speech in May 1989 in Nashville, Tennessee, at the end of a week of sales school with the Southwestern Company. I was 19 years old, and Mort Utley made one of the most unmotivational statements I had ever heard. He said:

"Most people do not get what they want out of life."

How depressing, I thought. This guy gets paid large amounts of money to motivate people and he comes on stage and says that most people do not get what they want out of life. My 19-year-old brain went "Thanks for the tip, Mort. I suppose next you'll tell me that people from France all speak French. No kidding, most people don't get what they want out of life. *Why do you think I am listening to you in the first place?*

I didn't want to be most people, and my guess is that you don't either. If you want to be most people—broke, unhealthy, and with too little time to actually enjoy your life—you wouldn't be reading this book. However, you have to be aware that your brain/mind has a lot of unconscious patterns that hold you back. Here's one of them.

**A big part of you wants just to be average**.

Starting in elementary school, through a combination of education and our brain's natural urge toward safety, we all develop a strong unconscious desire to be like everyone else around us. We want to fit in. We want to be average.

In America in 2012, here is what "average" really means.

- Physically—68 percent of Americans 20 and over are overweight; 34 percent are clinically obese. This average gets worse every year.
- Relationships—Over half of American marriages end in divorce, a statistic that's held for more than a quarter century.
- Professionally—Somewhere between 75 and 85 percent of Americans actively dislike their jobs.
- Financially—The average income in America hovers around $40,000, less than in the 1940s when adjusted for inflation. The average American saves less than $2,000 per year. Do the math: It means they can retire around age 96. Look around, and you'll see that at least half of American households regularly struggle with "too much month at the end of money."

And I could go on and on. Why do I start this way? Mainly because if you are serious in your quest to lead the kind of life that you really want, the first realization that needs to happen is that even now, in the most technologically advanced and prosperous society the world has ever seen, *average sucks!*

But as I said earlier, you don't want to be average. Congratulations! The fact that you are even reading this page indicates that average is not for you. You want to break records! In *Train Your Brain for Success* you are going to learn some fundamental principles, principles that have been proven over literally thousands of years to help individuals and organizations see consistent upward growth in every area—professionally, financially, physically, emotionally, spiritually, and in all types of relationships. The great thing about success it that it's simple. Not easy, but simple. Learn the fundamentals and apply them diligently, and you definitely will achieve the things you want.

So before we go further, I'd like you to do a short exercise. Consider whatever you believe to be your most important goal right now, and write it down.

Seriously, don't go any further until you've done this exercise. Whatever you consider to be your most important goal, please write it down.

Now look at what you wrote down, and envision that it has already happened. Imagine that you've made the money, that you've gotten the promotion, that you've lost the 20 pounds, or that you have the relationship that you have been looking for.

How does it feel? Good, right? I would suggest that what you currently have is a decent start. This book will show you how to take that thought seed that you have in front of you and transform it into something that doesn't just feel nice for a little while, but will actually cause you to *accomplish* that result—efficiently, joyfully, and with excitement.

We'll start with three mental factors for success. Understanding these concepts and applying them to any degree will automatically start you moving in the direction of your goals. The more you understand these, the faster and easier your goal achievement will become.

## Mental Factor Number One: Success Leaves Clues

This means that the achievement of your goals is not a function of magic, luck, or circumstances. It's a function of *how you think* and *what you do*. Look at the goal you wrote down earlier. Is there anybody, anywhere who has accomplished what you are looking to accomplish or better? I'm hard pressed to find anyone who can answer no to that question. Whatever you want to do, somebody has done it and that's very good news for you. If *anyone* else has accomplished what you are looking to accomplish, you can be totally confident that they didn't do it because they are somehow better or luckier than you. They did it because they thought a certain way and they took certain actions. If you'll develop the same thought patterns and the same habits it is virtually assured that you will end up in the same spot. Success leaves clues. So no matter where you're starting from, you have the ability to get where you want to go. It also means that one of the fastest ways to get where you want to go is to simply find somebody who's gotten there and copy what he or she did.

An excellent example of this concept is an interview I heard of with a very successful professional bass fisherman. This fisherman was known for winning fishing tournaments no matter how tough the bite was—he just caught fish all time even when nobody else did. So a reporter asked him, "How do you do it? How are you so successful at catching bass?" The pro's answer instructs that success leaves clues.

Fisherman: "Well, most folks think that bass fishing is all about luck. They think that if you happen to be at the right place at the right time with the right bait you'll catch fish, and if not... well, you won't. What I've learned is that bass fishing is much more predictable and scientific. On a given body of water, the time of year and the weather will pretty much tell you where the fish will be. Their location determines which presentations might work, so I just find the fish and experiment with a handful of lures and presentations until I find the one that works. Simple. Some days are tougher than others, but a systematic approach always works best."

Interviewer: "That sounds too easy—like anyone could do it."

Fisherman: "Yeah, that's probably true."

Interviewer: "Well then, why doesn't everyone catch fish as consistently as you?"

Fisherman: "Listen to the first thing I said. Most folks think that bass fishing is all about *luck*. They simply don't realize that they have so much influence, *so they never put in the time it takes to learn the patterns that work.* They just don't know."

This same is true about life. Yes—there are circumstances to deal with, and many are tough. But your success is not a function of those circumstances. It's a function of what you do with them. True, most people are not successful. Most people don't have the money, the relationships the health, or the life they really desire, because most of them think that they're just unlucky. Find successful people, people who are, who do, and who have what you want, and then do what they do. "Success leaves clues" means that success is something that can and should be modeled from others.

## Mental Factor Number Two: What You See Is What You Get

Most of the time when someone says "what you see is what you get" they're saying that nothing is hidden, that you can take a situation or person at face value. This is different. Here I mean that the pictures you see in your mind tend to be the results you get in your life. If you watch top-level athletes right before they perform—what are they doing? That's right, they're visualizing the outcome they want. They're seeing the ball go in the hole, they're seeing the perfect gymnastics routine—whatever their sport, they're seeing a perfect result—in their mind's eye.

Athletes do this is because they know *that it works.* Athletes understand that the more clearly they can picture their desired result, the more likely they are to deliver a performance that produces that result. Again, the same is true in your life—the more clearly you can picture the results you want, the more likely you are to deliver the performance that produces those results.

## Mental Factor Number Three: What You See Is What You Look For

The pictures that will live in your mind most consistently will probably be the pictures that you condition your mind to see. There is a very powerful part of your brain that can work either for you or against you. It's called the *Reticular Activating System (RAS)*, and it acts as a filter on your brain. It'll cause you to notice what you teach it to notice, and filter away almost everything else. You've experienced this part of your brain at work if you've ever made the decision to buy a particular kind of car. Think back to anytime you made the decision to buy a new car. As soon as you decided what you wanted, where did you start seeing that exact vehicle? That's right—everywhere! And that's not because they all of a sudden showed up in your environment; it's because you finally flipped the switch to notice them. And as soon as you flipped the switch you couldn't not notice them. The good news is you can use the reticular activating system for achieving your goals much more quickly and easily than you have. By the way, you'll see several references to the RAS throughout *Train Your Brain for Success*; it's very useful when used properly.

*Critical concept: Your brain is always working*. Your brain is either working for you or against you, but it's always working. And it's vital to understand that your brain's default setting for how it works is not very helpful. When it comes to your brain's natural tendencies, there's bad news, good news, and really good news.

## The Bad News: Your Comfort Zone Limits You

One of your brain's strongest tendencies is called the *homeostatic impulse*—the desire to stay where you are. More on this later, but your brain is highly evolved for survival; it is exceptionally good at keeping you alive. You may not like where you are right now, but the fact is that where you are right now has not killed you yet. As a result, your brain has deemed it safe, and will do all kinds of weird things to keep you there. Have you ever known someone who lost the same 20 pounds, four or five times? Have you known someone who paid off all their credit cards, only to rack them back up again? Or someone who had the same relationship with the same kind of person over and over again? All these are examples of this homeostatic impulse, popularly known as the Comfort Zone.

This is bad news because *no growth can occur in the Comfort Zone*. The only place you can grow is outside your Comfort Zone. I love this visual; see Figure I.1.

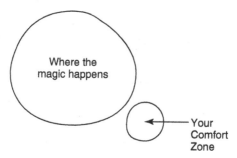

**Figure I.1** You Can Elevate Your Comfort Zone

Your Comfort Zone must be addressed if you want to see lasting change, because it's pull is incredibly strong.

## The Good News

Now that I've convinced you that you could be stuck forever right where you are (which you could), you must understand that this is not your destiny. You absolutely have the capacity to move your Comfort Zone to any place you'd prefer. Here's why:

*Whether you realize it or not, your Comfort Zone is something you have chosen.*

You've chosen it unconsciously, but you have chosen it. This is encouraging, because you have control over your choices. So you can consciously unchoose your current Comfort Zone and then choose differently. And the best part is that once you've elevated your Comfort Zone, your life stays elevated! You can permanently reset your internal thermostat to a higher level. It will require commitment, education, and a little help from outside yourself, but you absolutely can do it.

## The Really Good News: Small Changes Make a Huge Difference

You don't need to be 100 percent better to see a 100 percent improvement. You just need to be a little better. There's a concept in play here called the *winning edge*. It means that a small change in the right place makes a huge difference in the end result. In golf, a 1-mm difference in the angle of the club head means the difference between "middle of the fairway" and "you can't find your ball." In a horse race, the winning horse often wins "by a nose," but that split second is usually a fourfold increase in prize money. In sales, the tiniest perceived difference between competitors can mean the difference between receiving all of the business or none.

So take heart—small improvements in the right area of your life will give you a huge improvement in your end result. Here are some examples I've seen with my clients:

- An executive makes a small change in how he schedules his week and sees a $125,000 boost to his company's bottom line.
- A banking professional alters *one thing* about how she starts her day, and triples her income in six months.

- A salesperson simply pays attention to his forehead, and his results skyrocket.
- A teacher applies the simplest possible concept for Reading Smart, and his student goes from understanding almost none of what he reads to understanding almost all of it.

And I could go on and on. Ultimately, you get to choose how you use your brain. *Train Your Brain for Success* gives you the specific tools and skills to turn on your brain in a way that propels you forward.

## How to Use This Book

*Train Your Brain for Success* is not created as just a recreational, passive read. It's been set up to be:

1. An ongoing resource for your development.
2. A gateway into an entire system of accelerated learning and record-breaking results in your life.

In the first section, Your Learning Foundations, we'll tune up the most fundamental learning skills you possess—your Instant Recall Memory and your "Smart Reading" capacity. You'll be able to learn in a way that stimulates more of your brain and enables you to absorb any information more quickly and more permanently. Both of these sections are Memory Optimized™ with interactive video exercises that you'll find listed at the end of each chapter under Reinforcement and Bonuses. "Memory Optimized™" means that you'll literally be walked step by step through an easy, fun process for committing the main points to your long-term memory. Just follow the instructions and visit www.planetfreedom.com/trainyourbrain, using the access code found on page 232 of this book.

Read these sections first, and more importantly, do the Memory Optimization exercises that support the chapters. Will it take a little more time? Yes, on the front end. But the result will be that you will absorb the rest of the book much more efficiently and you'll remember it better. The best training in the world does you zero good if you don't apply it, and you can't apply it if you can't remember it. So get involved with your own learning.

The rest of *Train Your Brain for Success* will focus on the four components of record-breaking performance. Anytime an individual or an organization takes their results to a higher level, there are four things you can observe and then model.

1. Having energizing goals.
2. Being fully present; using time as it's meant to be used.
3. Being brilliant with basics.
4. Practicing aggressive mental care.

Chapters 7 through 18 are devoted to elevating your skills with these four components. In these chapters you'll develop specific plans for thinking and acting that are proven to get results quickly and in a way that lasts, in any important area of your life. Once again, these chapters are supported by exercises and tools that can be found under "Reinforcement and Bonuses." Read each chapter, take some notes, and then lock in your learning before going on to the next chapter. *Take an active approach to this book. Read it with a pen in your hand and a place to write your own thoughts.*

*You unquestionably can be, do, and have anything you want, but you can't do it with the thinking you've currently got.*

If you want a higher level of results, you must grow into a higher level of thinking. So many personal development books promise "the key" or "the secret" and then just tell you "you can do it!" That's fine, but we're going a step beyond. We're going to teach you how to get from point A to point B quickly, efficiently, and how to have a ball on the way!

# Section 1

## Your Learning Foundations

# Learning Foundation #1
# Your Instant Recall Memory

# 1

## Discovering Your
## Memory Power

A s we discussed in the Introduction, the first six chapters
of *Train Your Brain for Success* are dedicated to the very
foundations of your ability to learn, your ability to absorb and
then recall the information that you need for your growth. In
this section, you're going to learn how to learn in the way that
actually uses your brain in the way that it prefers to be used. Let's
start with one of the most popular subjects that my company
teaches: the subject of how to improve your memory.

Think for a moment about how many different ways you use
your memory on a daily basis. If you're having trouble coming
up with an answer, try this question on for size:

"If you lost your memory completely, what would you be
able to do?"

The correct answer is "nothing." When we're born, we
come into the world with a working autonomic nervous system,
so our breathing, heartbeat, and other bodily functions work
properly. And we have automatic reflexes, like when the doctor

hits your kneecap with that little rubber hammer to see if your muscles contract. That's it. Everything else in your life is learned. Even things as basic as what your own name is and how to eat are learned behaviors. So literally everything in your entire life requires the use of your memory.

Extend that out to your life today. At Freedom Personal Development, we will often ask our workshop audiences the question, "Where in your life do you feel an improved memory would help you be more effective, more productive, or reduce stress?" Just a few of the common answers we hear:

From professionals:

- "I wish I were better at remembering people's names!"
- "I wish I could deliver presentations without looking at notes!"
- "I wish I could learn product knowledge quicker!"
- "I wish I could remember dates and times for appointments!"

From students:

- "I wish I could remember foreign language vocabulary!"
- "I wish I could remember math formulas and equations!"
- "I wish I could remember things like the preamble to the Constitution, all the presidents, states, and capitals."
- "I wish I felt less freaked out when taking tests."

Honestly, I could just go on for an entire chapter about all the ways that we get to use our memories as tools for getting through life, so here's the best news:

No matter where you would like to see improvement in your memory or any area of learning, *you absolutely have the ability to make those improvements.* A significant body of research now confirms that for all practical purposes, your memory is actually perfect; you literally never "forget" anything. Some of you right now might be saying to yourself, "Okay, Roger, you just lost me.

I feel like I forget *stuff all the time!* Why do you think I bought this book in the first place?" And I understand that perception; I get where it *feels* that way. Fact is, though, that essentially everything—every book you've read, every conversation you've had, every person you've met—everything—is recorded by your brain. Your challenge is actually not your *memory*, but your *recall*.

Example: Think back to the last time you bumped into someone you knew (and you knew that you knew), but you couldn't come up with their name. Common situation, happens to everyone. See that instance in your mind. You probably had a reasonably good conversation with that person, right? Five or 10 minutes of "how's it going, how's work, how's the family," and so on. But the whole time you were talking to them, what was your brain doing? Racking itself with one question: "What the heck is this guy's name?" And it didn't come to you while he was there. *But it did come to you later.* See, you didn't forget that guy's name, you just couldn't *recall* it when you needed it.

Again, I could give you tons more examples, suffice it to say that your memory is in fact excellent, it's actually your recall that may be suspect. The reason this is good news is that improving your recall is very much under your control. If you can't recall a piece of information, it is always because the way that you stored it in the first place was accidental, mindless, haphazard, and unconscious. Here's what I mean.

## How You Originally Learned to Learn

If you're like 99 percent of the population, back in school you learned to learn through a process called *rote memorization*. Rote memorization is simply learning through repetition. You got some information (from a teacher or a textbook) and then went over it and over it and over it, until hopefully it stuck in your brain. Sound familiar?

How's that working for you now? Not too well, I would bet. Just to prove the point, take this short two-question quiz:

Question 1: Did you ever take a biology class?
        Yes_____ No_____
Question 2: Without looking it up, please name all the phyla of the animal kingdom.

In our live workshops, everyone says "of course" to question #1, and then nobody can even begin to answer #2. Which is fine; you don't actually need to know any of the phyla of the animal kingdom. The point is that if you took biology, I promise you were taught that information. The question is "did you actually learn it?", and the answer is almost assuredly no. You didn't *learn* that information, you *memorized* it for the test. Test came, you barfed the information up onto the test, and were done. Which was fine for back in school, but do you see the problem?

By following the process described above over and over again throughout your formalized education, you formed a habit of how you learn everything. My guess is that habit no longer serves you very well. Rote memorization actually can get you a decent grade on a test that you know is coming, but your life doesn't consist of tests that you know are coming, does it? So you'll need a method of learning that serves you a little better, which is exactly what you'll get from the first six chapters of *Train Your Brain for Success*, if you'll keep an open mind about your mind....

## The Teachability Index

*There is a specific way of thinking and acting for any result. Our job is to be open and flexible enough to adopt those ways of thinking and acting.*
    Bill Harris, founder of Centerpointe Research Institute

How much you get out of this book or any learning experience has a significant amount to do with you as a learner. This material will change your life, if and only if you absorb and apply it. So be aware of what's called your Teachability Index. It's a measurement of how ready you are to learn. Whether you realize it or not, the Teachability Index is in play anytime you are attempting to develop a new skill or a higher level of understanding of anything. There are two components of the Teachability Index, each of which can be easily evaluated on a scale of 1 to 10 (10 being the highest).

The first component of your Teachability Index is your *desire to learn*. It just makes sense that if you're going to maximize any learning experience you must want to learn what's being taught. Some of the best news about you as a learner is that your desire to learn is very high, like 9 or 10 on the scale. Congratulations! The reason I can say this with confidence is that even though you and I may have never met, I know for a fact that you've already made an investment in yourself. You've probably invested some money to buy this book (thanks!). Even if you didn't invest your own money for it, at a bare minimum you've invested some time to get this far. You simply wouldn't have made that investment if you didn't have a pretty darn strong desire to learn. So go ahead and grade your current desire to learn from 1 to 10.

Desire to learn score _____

The second component of the Teachability Index is a bit more tricky. It's called your *willingness to change*, and it cannot be taken for granted, ever. Anyone who attends one of our programs or picks up a book called *Train Your Brain for Success* inherently has a strong desire to learn. Nobody inherently has a strong willingness to change. It's because of the comfort zone we discussed in the introduction: We are hardwired to stay wherever we are and do whatever we have been doing, even if that behavior pattern isn't getting us the results our conscious mind wants. I'm not saying that you can't have a high willingness to change, because you can. I'm just saying that if you want to boost your willingness to change, you will need to do it consciously and purposely. It won't happen by accident. So what would you say is your current willingness to change score?

Willingness to change score _____

Now that you have some numbers, the correct way to gauge your Teachability Index is to multiply the two scores. The highest possible score is 100 (10 times 10). So why not do that now, just to see what you come out with.

Desire to learn score × willingness to change score = Total Teachability score

Notice that even if your desire to learn is a 10, if your willingness to change is a zero, your Total Teachability score is zero. For you to really learn, both scores need to be high. Don't just pay lip service to learning, do it! You picked up this book because you want your life to be better: true or false? Of course it's true, so if you really want that, you must do something different. The Chinese actually have defined insanity as "doing the same thing over and over and expecting a different result."

Lots of our clients have told us this is a useful exercise, anytime the objective is to learn something new. There's no need to be judgmental or upset, it's just helpful to notice. If someone has a higher Teachability Score than you, it does not make them better than you, but it does mean they will make progress faster than you.

All this is to say that for these chapters on memory training, I have one tip that will help you get maximum value from them.

Tip #1—*Don't judge the process*; *do evaluate the result.*

The method you'll learn here definitely produces results, but it is different than what you are accustomed to. Because it's different, your brain will likely give you a thought like "Well, this is just weird." Everyone who learns memory training goes through at least one phase where they just think the whole thing is just a goofy bag of tricks. It's not. So when you experience that thought, I recommend you check your Teachability Index, get over it, and keep moving forward. So don't waste time or energy trying to pick apart or analyze the process; there's plenty of time for that later if it's of interest to you. You'll learn much more quickly if you *don't judge the process.*

At the same time, *do evaluate your results.* That's how you're evaluated in your profession, isn't it? Do the same thing here: Trust the process, engage in what I ask you to engage in, and just see how it works. My guess is you'll impress yourself with how quickly you can boost your abilities.

Tip #2—*Have fun with your brain!* One of the things we know for sure is that at its best, learning is fun. There are a couple of aspects to this.

First off, think about the sense of enjoyment you feel when you learn anything new. Ever waterskied? Snowboarded? Played backgammon? Figured out how to sell something? Conquered a fear? When you started "getting it," it felt good, right? Whether or not you liked school, your brain likes to learn new things!

Secondly, we know that your brain's stress response—fight or flight—is clearly the worst possible state for learning something new. It's very effective if you've already been trained in something and you've reached a level of unconscious competence, but for learning new skills or information, the fight or flight stress response essentially shuts that ability down immediately. The whole reason you remembered that guy's name later is that after he left your presence you *took a deep breath and relaxed.* While he was there and you were racking your brain, your brain was experiencing the same thing that soldiers experience in battle! Granted, it was milder (the grocery store is a less intense scene than the battlefield), but fundamentally the biochemistry and brainwave activity are the same.

In our workshops we teach that *stress is the #1 killer of your mental ability.* So back off on the pressure a little. If you get stuck or stumped, just take a deep breath, tell yourself "This will come to me," and move on. Come back to it later. That's often all you need to re-fire some neurons that will get you where you want to go.

Just be open-minded about your mind. If you're anything like the hundreds of thousands of people who've experienced our live workshops, you are capable of way more than you think you are. So let's have some fun.

## Your Baseline Memory Evaluation

Before we leave this chapter, let's just see where you're starting from. In a few moments, you're going to see a list of 20 items. Your job is to look the list over as slowly and carefully as you can, for no more than five minutes. Do the best job you can to commit the list to memory in that time span. You are not allowed to write the items down on scratch paper, only use your mind. When you are done, flip to the test on the next page and without looking back, write down the 20 items in order to the best of your ability. Ready? Go.

| | |
|---|---|
| a unicorn | chopsticks |
| an electrical outlet | a rose |
| a tricycle | a black cat |
| a truck | gold |
| a hand | a dollar sign |
| a can of beer | a candle |
| a hockey stick | a wizard |
| a spider | a golf green |
| a baseball | a sauna |
| a dime | a dartboard |

Again, take no more than five minutes to study the list. Once you're done, go to the next page and write down those 20 items, in order, without looking back at this page. Go.

————————          ————————
————————          ————————
————————          ————————
————————          ————————
————————          ————————
————————          ————————
————————          ————————
————————          ————————
————————          ————————
————————          ————————
————————          ————————
————————          ————————
————————          ————————
————————          ————————
————————          ————————
————————          ————————

How'd you do? If you're like most of our students, not so well. When we do this exercise in a live workshop, the average score is about 6 out of 20. If you did better than that, congratulations. If not, don't worry about it. Your score for the baseline evaluation is actually irrelevant, except as a baseline. There are a couple of great lessons to take away about some of your brain's natural tendencies that can be *harnessed.*

## Tendency #1—The Rule of 7, Plus or Minus 2

Without a system, your brain can only handle a maximum of five to seven pieces of information at a time (and often it's more like three to five). If you were just trying to learn that list of 20 items through rote memory, one pattern you likely realized is that you did pretty well with the first five to seven on the list and then began to struggle. If this happened, don't worry; it doesn't mean there's something wrong with you, it just means you were operating without a system. When you do that, you're bound by your memory's inability to handle more than a handful of different pieces.

By the way, if you did get more than seven of the items, I would bet money that you were doing something other than just rote memorization. It does happen in our live workshops where some people will score ten or more on the baseline evaluation, and they are never doing it with rote memorization. They either made an acronym, created some kind of story out of the items, or noticed the pattern in the list that I'll teach you in a minute. Rest assured, without some kind of technique or system, your brain can only deal effectively with about seven items, plus or minus two.

## Tendency #2—Primacy and Recency

One of the most common patterns we see on this baseline quiz is called *primacy and recency*. This means that with a bunch of information to remember, your brain will naturally be effective with the information at the beginning and the end, while struggling in the middle. Again, it doesn't mean you're broken—primacy and recency is just natural tendency.

Understanding these tendencies leads us to our most basic recall improvement principle: chunking. It simply means that you will automatically improve your brain's ability to recall if you will break things into bite-sized pieces. If you would have seen the baseline quiz like this:

a unicorn
an electrical outlet
a tricycle
a truck
a hand

a can of beer
a hockey stick
a spider
a baseball
a dime

chopsticks

a rose

a black cat

gold

a dollar sign

a candle

a wizard

a golf green

a sauna

a dartboard

Your performance would have improved. Why? More beginnings and more ends! Just this one concept can be a huge help for your brain. When you learn anything, take it in bite-sized chunks as much as possible. That's bite-sized chunks of information and bite-sized chunks of time. Even with this book, I recommend you read no more than one chapter at a time. When you finish a chapter, take a moment to review what was covered, in writing or at least in your mind. Take a quick stretch break, grab a drink of water, get your mind off of the book for a few minutes. Then and only then come back to reading. You'll get way more out of it.

Okay, now that we've got your baseline score and a baseline understanding of how your brain operates naturally, let's supercharge it. In the next two chapters, you're going to learn how to speak the language of your brain, mentally organize information of all kinds, and improve your recall for any number of applications. Let's go!

**Reinforcement and Bonuses:** This chapter has been Memory Optimized™ for your benefit. For your brief lesson and some great bonuses, visit www.planetfreedom.com/trainyourbrain with the access code on page 232. Enjoy!

# 2

# Learn to Speak the Language of Your Memory!

Did you know that your memory has a language? We touched on it in the introduction, when we talked about "what you see is what you get." The language of your memory (and every other function of your brain) is *images*. One of the other default settings of your learning capacity that can be harnessed is your brain's powerful tendency and ability to see images. The more you can visualize information, the easier it is to recall.

Some good news is that you already think in images. You may not have realized it consciously, but you do. If I asked you to recall 50 things about your living room right now, what would you do? That's right, you would just see a *mental image* of your living room! By doing so, you'd be able to recall tons of detail, even though you've never memorized your living room. Learn to trust that ability—we're going to start developing it right now.

Let's redo that baseline test, only with a small twist.

1. unicorn
2. electrical outlet
3. tricycle
4. truck
5. hand

6. beer
7. hockey stick
8. spider
9. baseball
10. dime

11. chopsticks
12. roses
13. black cat
14. gold
15. dollar sign

16. candles
17. wizard
18. golf green
19. sauna
20. dartboard

Okay, two twists: We broke it up, and now we've got numbers. This "unicorn list" is the same baseline test we start all of our memory training workshops with, and here's what we find. Seeing/knowing the numbers with each item can, all by itself, create an association that's beneficial. See it? Most of the numbers do have a logical connection with the item that represents them —1 and unicorn, 3 and tricycle, 12 (a dozen) roses. In fact, the technique you're learning right now is called *basic association*, and it's a valid technique *to begin with*. Infinitely more valuable, however, is when you create a vivid image of each item in your mind. Even without a logical association (for example #15 is a stretch, #17 is really a stretch, and there is none at all for #19), the image is what your brain needs. So you'll take the test again, but first follow the simple directions. You're going to walk through the exact same 20 items, but this time you're going to see the images in your mind as vividly and clearly as you can. Let me emphasize: See the images as vividly and clearly as you can. Don't just say "ya, I got it." Just take a few seconds with each one, then take the test on page 20. See these images in your mind, and study for no more than three minutes.

1. See a brilliant white *unicorn* with his *1* horn.
2. See the beige *electrical outlet* with its *2* slots.
3. See the red *tricycle* with its *3* black rubber wheels and a *3*-year-old kid on it.
4. See the *truck* with its *4* wheels, its *4* doors, and the *for* sale sign in the window.
5. See your *hand* with its *5* fingers.
6. See that *6*-pack of *beer* (you choose your favorite brand).
7. See the wooden *hockey stick* shaped like a *7.*
8. See that big black *spider* with its *8* legs.
9. See that round *baseball* being tossed around by the *9* players on the field for *9* innings.
10. See that *10* cents, the thin, silver, shiny *dime*.

Let me just pause for a moment to let you review in your mind the images you just created, and remind you to see these images as clearly and vividly as you can. Moving on:

11. See those thin *chopsticks* that look like the number *11* being pulled out of their wrapper.
12. See those *12* beautiful red *roses* in a bouquet.
13. See that *black cat* on Friday the *13th*.

14. Vividly see that *14*-carat *gold* coin (or bar or nugget or ring; you choose).

15. Take the two digits of number *15* and squeeze them together into a *dollar sign*.

16. See *16* flaming *candles* on a birthday cake. Maybe even sing the song . . .

17. See that young *wizard* with the round glasses graduating from Hogwarts at age *17*. (I said it was a stretch).

18. See that *golf green* with its perfectly cropped green grass on the *18th* hole.

19. See *19* sweaty guys in that *sauna*. (I said there's no logical connection, but you're seeing it anyway, aren't you?)

20. See that round, light-up *dartboard* with the *20* scoring stripes and the number *20* on the top.

Now take a moment to review in your mind and see the images vividly and clearly. Ready? Now go to the next page and without looking back, write down the 20 items on the unicorn list. If you get stuck on one, don't freak out, just skip it and come back to it a little later. Go for it.

1. _____

2. _____

3. _____

4. _____

5. _____

6. _____

7. _____

8. _____

9. _____

10. _____

11. _____

12. _____

13. _____

14. _____

15. _____

16. _____

17. _____

18. _____

19. _____

20. _____

How did it go this time? Better, I would guess. In our live workshops, the average score the second time through jumps from about six to about 18, and most everyone gets them all. Why?

First off: True it's the second time through, which is an automatic advantage. You also do have that logical numerical connection for most of the items, which also helps. Most importantly, however, you created a vivid image for each of the items—you actually spoke the language of your memory. Just for kicks, take one more quick quiz:

Without looking back, what was:

#4?

#8?

#17?

What # was:

Sauna?

Dime?

Dollar Sign?

See? Even out of order, those images serve you well!

## Two Plusses and One Big Minus of What You Just Did

There are two things in that baseline exercise that are really useful for training your brain, and one really big problem. What's useful is that, if you played along, you first started using the visual centers of your brain more purposefully, and second, you probably gained some confidence.

Both of those are really significant for your progress, more so than you probably realize right now,

*The big problem is that the whole list was rigged.* I am aware of that. I am also aware that life doesn't usually hand you information in a way that works quite as conveniently as when "4 just happens to be a truck" and "11 just happens to be chopsticks." But are *you* aware now of just how quickly you can make progress with just a little bit of training? Does that build your confidence at least a little? It should. I mean, who knew you were such a genius?

It's true however, that because life very rarely gives you people's names, details of conversations, or any other information prepackaged with such convenient associations, you will want something that can deliver *instant recall.* If you can remove the need for a logical connection, you then develop the tools for remembering literally anything at any time. That's next.

## The Mental File Folder System

I want you to imagine right now that you are in the office of a Fortune 500 company. You and I are standing in front of a filing cabinet that's filled with the files of every client this company has. There are literally hundreds of thousands of files, organized alphabetically by last name. Now I want you to imagine that I've asked you to get:

- your file,
- my file, and
- some guy named Arturo Rodriguez's file.

Would you be able to find those files quickly? Of course you would—why?

Because *there's a system* for organizing this information.

You may have thought "because it's alphabetical," which is also true. I said the information was organized alphabetically, but fundamentally the reason you'd be able to locate those three files (or any number of files for that matter) quickly is just that there *is a system*. Your brain is *designed* to operate on the same principal, with an organizational system in place. A huge part of why you have trouble recalling the stuff you have trouble recalling is simply that nobody's ever taught you how to organize information mentally. The opportunity here is that when you do develop an organizational system for your brain and then speak the (visual) language of your memory, you become so effective at storing and recalling information that you gain a huge competitive advantage.

Here's how we do it:

It's called the Mental File Folder System, aka the F.I.G. system. F.I.G. is an acronym (also a very helpful memory technique) that represents the three things you need to develop instant recall of anything, from names to presentations to this book to a grocery list to where you left your keys. It's awesome.

**F stands for File**

**I stands for Image**

**G stands for Glue**

Get a good clear mental image of a fig. If you don't know what a fig looks like, visualize a Fig Newton. Either one works perfectly. Let's break these down.

### F is for File

The first thing necessary for instant recall is a *file*, which is just a place to store information. We've already discussed this concept, so what can you use as a mental file? *Anything you can see.* Anything you can see with your eyes, or just with your mind's eye can work as a terrific place to store information. Your home, your office, your car, your body, and so on. Literally anything that you can see can be used as a place to store information. In this book, you'll get two filing systems in place.

### I is for Image

We've already discussed at length how the language of your memory is *images.* Just in case you're still not getting this concept, consider this. Faces are much easier to remember than names, right? How many times have you seen someone and said, "I recognize the face, but I can't recall the name"? It never goes the other way. You've never seen someone and said "Hey, you're Roger Seip, but I forgot your face!" Your brain loves images, so the more clearly and vividly you can visualize information, the easier it is to recall later.

### G is for Glue

Here's where the magic happens. Once you have a file to store information and then have it in a vivid image format, you'll want to *glue* the image to the file so that it sticks. What makes for strong glue? Two things.

### Action and Emotion

The more *action* and *emotion* involved with your images, the better they will stick to your files.

Here's a good example of this: Can you remember every time you've driven your car? Of course not, but you *can* remember the times you got in an accident or got pulled over, right? Why? Lots of action and emotion. Can you remember where you were or what you were doing on August 11, 2001? Probably not, but

I bet you can remember your life in vivid detail on *September* 11, 2001. Why? Lots of action and emotion.

How do you harness this? When you're creating mental images and gluing them to your files, make the images as action-oriented as possible. Make them as vivid, crazy, and outlandish as possible. Images that are doing something are much more effective than images that are just sitting there. A client of mine once said "Your brain remembers videos better than snapshots." Images that make you laugh, gross you out, seem totally ridiculous, or are even kind of racy work much better than images that make logical sense but are boring or normal. Every world champion memory athlete (yes, there are memory championships, and the competitors are amazing in what they can do) will tell you that when it comes to creating images that are memorable, "It's helpful to have kind of a dirty mind." So incorporate as much action and emotion into your images as possible.

You'll see examples of this vivid action and emotion as we progress.

### Your First Filing System—Your Body

What did we say can be used as a file? Anything you can see with your eyes or visualize with your mind. The first file system we usually create in our workshops is called your body files. It's a great first system because:

- You can see it.
- It's always with you.
- You know the parts of your body without much thought, so it's easy.

Right here you're going to get the same body files we create in our live workshops, using the exact same order and the exact same terminology. Just because of space limitations, I won't go into all the specific reasons why we use this order and this terminology, but rest assured there is a specific reason. Again, don't judge the process, do evaluate your results. You'll use 10 body files, in the following order:

1. Your **soles** (of your feet)
2. Your **shins**
3. Your **legs**
4. Your **butt**
5. Your **tummy**

Note: Your tummy creates what we call a center or midpoint file. We're halfway through this list of 10 files. Notice you are also approximately halfway up your body. This creation of a center file is not necessary, but it's really helpful as it takes advantage of the principle of chunking. We recommend it every time you create a filing system. Onward:

6. Your **ribs**
7. Your **collarbone**
8. Your **mouth**
9. Your **nose**
10. Your **forehead**

Take a moment to review these in your mind, even physically touch each one of them in order. Now, to lock them in, go to the next page and write them down. Do it without looking back, and do the best you can. If you get stuck on the name of one or two files, don't worry. Just skip over those and get the ones you can. Once you're to the end, see if your brain gave you the ones you may have missed. If you're just blank, come back to this page for the answers.

Body File #1 _____
Body File #2 _____
Body File #3 _____
Body File #4 _____
Body File #5 _____
Body File #6 _____
Body File #7 _____
Body File #8 _____
Body File #9 _____
Body File #10 _____

Just to double-lock them in, please write them down in reverse order. This time no looking back at all.

10

9

8

7

6

5

4

3

2

1

Nice work! You've now got an excellent filing system in place! I've seen our clients use their body files as a terrific place to store all kinds of important information—grocery lists, to-do lists, huge charts full of numerical data, foreign languages, you name it. In Chapter 3 we'll be using your body files (along with another filing system you've already developed but probably didn't realize it) to visually learn all the main points found here in *Train Your Brain for Success*, as well as some other applications that will boost your mental capacity on a number of different levels.

Before we move on, I wanted to give you a little encouragement about learning in general. I'm aware that what you're doing right now is probably quite a bit different from what you're accustomed to doing with a book. Because it's different, you may feel a little awkward or uncomfortable with the process at this point. That may even continue for a little while. So here are four things to wrap up this chapter.

1. If you're feeling a little awkward, understand that is a normal and required part of learning something new.

2. I told you this awkwardness and discomfort could happen, and I also told you that you will break through. *Don't judge the process; do evaluate your results*. Sometimes results come quickly, sometimes they take a little longer. Everyone learns at their own pace.

3. I'm sure you've heard the saying that anything worth doing is worth doing well. Brian Tracy taught me that anything worth doing is worth doing *poorly*, at first. Seriously, think about anything you're good at now and that you love. You had to go through a learning curve with it just like anything else. If learning more effectively is important to you, embrace that learning curve when it comes to improving your recall and your life.

4. Depending on your learning style, you may just learn some skills better from seeing something done than by reading it in a book. That's why we've created the Reinforcement and Bonuses. Don't hesitate to use those for a fully interactive visual training reinforcement.

I also think it's appropriate to give you and your brain a little recognition. If you've done this chapter in the way that

I've asked, you've likely spent somewhere between 30 and 60 minutes working through it. That's not much time, and look at how much improvement you've already made! The first time you tested yourself on the unicorn list, you got a handful of correct answers. Now, just from this one chapter, you've probably got:

- All 20 items on the unicorn list.
- A working knowledge of the language of your memory.
- A basic understanding of the mental file folder system.
- Three things needed to remember anything: File, Image, Glue.
- Ten body files that are primed and ready to store information.

That's 35 separate pieces of information, in a relatively short period of time. Congratulations! You may be realizing that your brain is capable of way more than you thought just a few hours ago. As a brain training tool, we strongly encourage you to frequently catch yourself doing things right. Don't BS yourself, but when you give yourself little mental pats on the back, you're activating the reward centers in your brain in a way that boosts your energy and makes you crave more learning. You'll learn all about "Little Victories" in Chapter 17, but reinforce those reward centers starting now—you deserve it!

With that in mind, let's start loading useful information into those files!

**Reinforcement and Bonuses:** This chapter has been Memory Optimized™ for your benefit. For your brief lesson and some great bonuses, visit www.planetfreedom .com/trainyourbrain with the access code on page 232. Enjoy!

# 3

# Using Your New Mental Files with This Book and Beyond

Now that you've got some places to store information, it's time to get your brain revved up and store some information there. We'll start with one of the simplest examples we teach, which is a simple shopping list. It's a good one to start with, because the items are concrete and tangible, plus you'll be able to use the technique lots of times.

You need to hit the grocery store, and here's what you need to get.

- Oil (specifically, fish oil and flax oil)
- Avocados
- Walnuts
- Salmon
- Spinach
- Blueberries
- Beans
- Broccoli

- Some form of superfruit (pomegranate, acai, mangosteen, or the like; more on this in a bit)
- Green tea
- Yogurt
- Vitamins

Before we do this exercise, here are two keys to maximizing the effectiveness and efficiency of any mental filing system:

*Key #1*—Always start from the same file, and always go in the same order. Don't waste even one iota of energy trying to determine where the most logical place to file something is. Your brain doesn't care! Whatever is first on the list goes on the first file. One of the keys to developing speed is to streamline your thinking. So just do it in order.

*Key #2*—Use strong glue, and lots of it. The more action you give your images, the more vivid and crazy you make them, the stickier they will be.

Since it's your first shot, I'll guide you up your files. Here we go.

1. On your soles—see oil (specifically fish oil and flax oil) gooshing all over them.
2. On your shins—take an avocado and smoosh it all over them.
3. On your legs—crush some walnuts between them.
4. On your butt—see yourself sitting on a salmon.
5. On your tummy—fill up your tummy with spinach.

(By now you should know that halfway through is a great time to review, so take a moment and mentally review the images you have on those files.)

6. On your ribs—see enormous blueberries jumping around staining your ribs purple.
7. On your collarbone—see beans jumping all around.

8. On your mouth—jam a stalk of broccoli in it.

9. On your nose—see Superman eating some fruit.

10. On your forehead—sits a green teapot full of yogurt and vitamins.

Take a moment and review what you see on those files and now quiz yourself:

**Body Files Grocery List Quiz: What did you store on your:**

1. (Soles) _____

2. (Shins) _____

3. (Legs) _____

4. (Butt) _____

5. (Tummy)_____

6. (Ribs) _____

7. (Collarbone) _____

8. (Mouth) _____

9. (Nose) _____

10. (Forehead) _____

Good job! Notice how even without any logical association, the images that you vividly visualize with action and emotion stick to those files really well. When we teach this technique in our live courses, the same questions always come up. Let's answer the most common ones before we move into some more applications.

### Question #1: What if I have more than 10 or 12 items?

Two answers:

First off, notice how easy it is to see multiple items on one given file (your soles and your forehead each had multiples). As long as you visualize well, it's not difficult for your brain to handle this. So even with just these ten body files, you could literally store dozens, even hundreds of pieces of information. For example, I helped teach a Sunday School class of 40 middle-schoolers all 66 books of the Bible using just 10 files.

The other possibility is that you can certainly create more files for yourself. Ten is just a great number of files to start with; you may want to expand it. See the bonus material at the end of this chapter for some great tips.

### Question #2: How do I delete information?

Honestly, I just wouldn't worry about this too much. There are occasions where you might find it counterproductive to retain information beyond a certain time frame, but natural processes just take care of it. In a case like this, simply do not review your list. Because of the principles of primacy and recency, you will default to having the easiest recall of the most recent information you've filed. If you really feel the need to not remember something, you can just visualize an item being taken off a file and it shouldn't bother you anymore.

The bigger question here is usually the opposite: "How do I retain information for the long term?" Long-term recall is important enough that we've devoted a whole section of this chapter to it: See it under "The key to long-term recall" toward the end of this chapter.

### Question #3: Can I use the same filing system to hold multiple sets of information simultaneously?

Answer: Absolutely—you just need to give your list a title. We're going to do it in the next exercise. Just watch.

Let's tie these questions together with another application of your body files. We did "body files shopping list." Now we'll do "body files to-do list." It will be a little smaller list (we'll do just six items), but you'll get the point. This time, just see these images vividly. I'll give you the meaning of the images once you've got them.

1. On your soles, see an oxygen mask.
2. On your shins, see running shoes.
3. On your legs, see a balance beam with someone doing yoga on it.
4. On your butt, see a brain doing push-ups, jumping jacks, and other forms of exercise.
5. On your tummy, see a chalkboard.
6. On your ribs, see a pillow.

Now without looking, take the short quiz:

**Body Files To-Do List Quiz: What did you store on your:**
1. (Soles)_____
2. (Shins)_____
3. (Legs)_____
4. (Butt)_____
5. (Tummy)_____
6. (Ribs)_____

Did you get most of them? I bet you did, and I want you to notice something else. With each exercise, are you seeing where I'm giving you fewer clues? Pay attention to that; your brain is already experiencing a training effect where it's doing more and more on its own, without help.

So to directly answer Question #4 above, just try this little quiz:

On the grocery list, where would you find walnuts? _____
To-do list, where would you find a balance beam? _____
Grocery list, what's in your mouth? _____
To-do list, what's on your ribs? _____
Grocery list, where would you find spinach? _____
To-do list, what's on your tummy? _____

We could do this all day, couldn't we? Notice how, as long as you've titled your lists, your brain does an excellent job of keeping them separate. We've used your body files twice; you can do the same thing dozens of times simultaneously without fear of getting crossed up.

## Taking Optimal Care of Your Brain

Part of why you're getting these particular lists is that they point up a critical aspect of training your brain: proper maintenance and feeding of the organ itself. We've taught for years that your mind and your brain are much like a muscle. The better you exercise and feed it, the stronger it gets and the longer it stays healthy. There's an enormous body of research that now explains why and how this works. I'll give you the short version here; not everyone reading this book cares to know all the science.

(Some of you will find it fascinating. If you crave a more detailed explanation of the science, see the Reinforcement and Bonus section at the end of this chapter.)

Take a look at the items on the grocery list. What you've got are 13 foods that are known to have a positive impact on brain health. The first five (the two kinds of oil, avocado, walnuts, and salmon) contain high levels of the *Omega 3 fatty acids*, which essentially insulate the electrical circuitry in your brain. The rest of them—spinach, blueberries, beans of all kinds, broccoli, the superfruits, green tea, yogurt, and vitamins contain high levels of various *antioxidants*, which not only impact your brain but your cardiovascular system. Proportionally, your brain uses about 10 times more oxygen than any other part of your body, so anything that's good for your heart is also good for your brain. Yogurt also happens to be one of the best sources of healthy bacteria in your digestive system. Dr. Mark Hyman was one of the first to uncover the massive connection between digestive health and brain health, and more is being learned about this connection all the time.

The same concept applies to your to-do list. You've got images there that represent activities that are known to boost brainpower.

- The oxygen mask for *good breathing*. We've already talked about how one or two deep breaths alleviate that fight or flight response that shuts off learning. Regular deep breathing oxygenates the blood and boosts the overall capacity of your brain.

- The running shoes represent *aerobic exercise*. What's good for the heart is good for the brain.

- The balance beam with the yogi on it. We now know that *any form of physical exercise involving balancing* (yoga is the most popular form, and there are many others) does specific things to strengthen neural pathways.

- That brain doing exercise just symbolizes *mental exercise*. Activities that challenge your mind (think crosswords, sudoku, Words with Friends, etc.) literally are like weight workouts for your brain.

- The chalkboard represents *overall learning*. Research on healthy people in their eighties and beyond shows that they share two common traits. They have a strong sense of community with other people, and they are still learning new things. A life commitment to personal development—reading, listening to educational audios, sharing ideas with successful people, and so on—actually makes your brain healthier.

- The pillow represents *sleep*. We now know that being poorly rested and sleep deprived has some of the same effects on mental performance as excess alcohol. A good night's rest is one of the very best ways to boost brain health.

Again, entire volumes have been devoted to each one of the points listed above. Our "resident expert" on the issue of optimal brain maintenance is also our top-rated instructor, Tom Weber. If you'd like more science, check out Tom's video. If you don't care about the science and just want a stronger brain, simply start incorporating more of the above foods and activities into your life. Your brain will thank you for it.

## Your Next Filing System

Earlier I promised that you'd come out of your experience reading *Train Your Brain for Success* with two filing systems. We've been doing all this work with the body files, so you may be wondering "What's the second one gonna be?" You already learned it. Remember what we said you can use as a filing system? Anything you can see with your eyes or with your mind's eye.

Go back in your mind to the unicorn list we created in the last chapter. Can you see it in your mind? What was #1? How about #6? #18? What number is a candle? How about a spider? A truck? You can see it clearly now, can't you? The unicorn list itself makes an excellent filing system, plus it comes preloaded with numbers.

Let's have some fun and try it out. Now that your brain is primed up with those unicorn list images, see the following images in your mind as vividly as possible. Seriously, go a little nuts with your visualizations here (nobody will know). Take the following scenarios and play them out mentally, maybe even using some of the images like animated cartoons. Take as much time as you need to see these images, then take the short quiz on page 39.

1. A *unicorn discovering* that he has the words *memory power* spray painted on him in bright red printed letters.
2. An *electrical outlet*, speaking a foreign *language*, from *memory*.
3. Riding a *tricycle* into a huge *filing cabinet*, sending files flying everywhere.

4. A classroom full of *sixth-graders*, *reading* in a *truck*.

5. Your *hand*, holding a bunch of *tools*.

6. *Reading* a can of *beer*, drinking it, and *retaining* all of it forever.

7. A *hockey stick* shooting five different *characters* into a *goal*.

8. A *spider* holding *a magnifying glass*. The magnifying glass is focusing on a *key* and a *stone*.

9. An enormous *baseball* (like 100 feet tall), rolling over an *obstacle course*.

10. A *dime* studying Greek *mythology*, then wondering what *time* his *manager* would be in?

11. Using *chopsticks* for *two hours*. You're using them for the purpose of *smashing record* albums.

12. A dozen *roses*, *charging* up *Superman*.

13. A *black cat* eating an apple *core*. Not the whole apple, just the *core*.

14. A massive *gold coin* riding on top of a *porpoise* (not a dolphin, a *porpoise*). This porpoise has excellent *vision*, and it's on a special *mission*.

15. A huge statue of a *dollar sign*, glowing with a huge surplus of *energy*.

16. An enormous red, white, and blue *candle* with *five* separate *tools* that you pull out of it. This candle then uses these tools to fix up a *manger*.

17. A *wizard* holding an *hourglass* with the word "*power*" written all over it in *neon pink*.

## Quiz:

1. What did the unicorn discover?

2. What was the electrical outlet speaking?

3. What did you smash into with your tricycle?

4. What were those sixth-graders doing in that truck?

5. What were you holding in your hand?

6. What were the three things you did with that can of beer?

7. What was the hockey stick shooting into the goal? How many were there?

8. What was the spider holding? And what was it focusing on?

9. What was the huge baseball rolling over?

10. What was your dime studying? And what did it then wonder?

11. How long did you use the chopsticks? And what were you using them for?

12. The roses were charging up which hero?

13. The black cat was eating which part of what fruit?

14. What was the gold coin riding on? What sense did this creature have very strongly?

15. Why was the dollar sign glowing?

16. How many tools did the candle use? What was it fixing?

17. What was that wizard holding in his hands? What word was written all over it?

Have you figured out what that crazy little exercise just helped you remember in just a few minutes? Go back and look at the Contents right now. Notice the numbers of the chapters and the key words that name each one. That's right, you just memorized the titles of all 17 chapters in *Train Your Brain for Success*, in the exact right numerical sequence. Your memory optimized this book—Congratulations!

## The Key to Long-Term Recall: Spaced Repetition

There are an awful lot of instances where you learn something and it's critical to be able to retain it for the long term—weeks, months, or even years. If you want to retain information for the long term, I've once again got bad news, good news, and really good news.

The bad news is that you will need to review. Yes, there will be some effort required on your part. All of this ultimately is a skill, not a magic trick. So you will need to spend some time focusing and reviewing if you want information to stick long term.

The good news here is that you don't need to review incessantly. Kids and adults alike usually make studying way more stressful and time-consuming than it should be. To lock information in long term, follow the spaced repetition protocol: one hour, one day, one week. Whenever you identify something you want your brain to hold onto for more than 24 hours, simply review it mentally within approximately:

- **One hour**, while it's still fresh in your mind.
- **One day**, after you've slept and had a significant time with a different focus.
- **One week**; if you revisit information five to seven days later, the neural pathway for long-term recall really starts to get cemented.

For a little extra insurance feel free to spend a little time with information beyond a week; I usually recommend a review shortly before performing. For example, a quick mental review of the names of people in a meeting right before that meeting; reviewing a presentation you're about to give; or a student reviewing material before an exam. My point here is that you don't need to be constantly reviewing to retain information long term. Spaced repetition is the key.

The really good news is that you can effectively review anything in a very short period of time. Throughout these chapters on memory training, I've actually quizzed you several times with a technique called *random practice*. By reviewing in random order (instead of sequentially), your brain does a ton of effective work in very little time. Let's just do it.

**Pop Quiz (just do this in your mind—no need to write the answers):**
On your unicorn list, what was:
#8?
#3?
#16?
A dime?
An electrical outlet?
A sauna?

Pause for a moment—did you just review six of the 20 items? Yes, but in order to do it in random order *your brain actually reviewed all 20 items six times, in a matter of seconds.*

**Now onto your body files:**
What were your first, fourth, and eighth body files?
On your grocery list, what was on your:
Legs?
Butt?
Nose?
On your to-do list, what was on your:
Soles?
Tummy?

**Extra credit:**
What is Chapter 9 in this book called?
How about Chapter 3?

If you need to look up the answers, feel free to do so. My guess though is that you don't need to. You're seeing this information in your mind, and are you noticing the speed at which your brain works? To review all that information, how long did it take? A few minutes? Maybe less than a minute? *Your brain loves speed*—harness that capability when you review.

# Remembering Names

By far the most popular request that we get in terms of memory training applications is the issue of remembering the names of important people you meet. It's an important skill, because names are so personal. Dale Carnegie said, "The sweetest sound to anyone's ears is the sound of their own name." So true—the simple ability or inability to remember a name can have a major impact on all kinds of relationships. In our live and online workshops we spend hours on this topic. In this format, you can massively improve your ability to remember names with just a few easy practices.

### Short Term

There are two general categories of being unable to recall someone's name. The first is the short term. Have you ever met someone, shook their hand, got their name, and then five seconds later you couldn't recall their name? This is where the vast majority of names get dropped. Here's effectively the cure: When you're meeting someone for the first time,

1. Stop, clear your mind, and listen. The reason you lose names in five seconds is not that you have a bad memory but that you're a bad listener! It happens because your brain thinks about seven times faster than people speak, so it's easy for it to wander to all kinds of thoughts while a new person is telling you their name. You only have about five seconds to make a first impression on someone, so consciously invest as much of those five seconds as possible in one and only one thing: listening to the name you're hearing.

2. Repeat the person's name back to them, out loud, two or three times. Don't be ridiculous about it; if you met me and said "Roger, Roger, Roger," I would never want to speak with you again. But if you met me and said "Roger, nice to meet you, Roger," that would do a ton to help lock in my name quickly and be a natural part of the conversation.

## Long Term

The other issue is long-term. Ever seen someone you knew (and you knew that you knew), but couldn't come up with their name? That's long term. To stay out of this scenario, train yourself to:

- Review the names of people you meet using spaced repetition. At the end of a conversation, use their name. "It's been a pleasure meeting you, Dave" does way more for your memory than just "Bye." At the end of the day take a moment to refresh yourself on who you met that day. At the end of the week, take five minutes and review those names once more. This is exactly how our instructors can have 200 people they've met over a six-month period show up for a workshop and remember all of their names. A little review goes a long way.
- Visualize names: Turn them into images! Some names are already images—Rose, Crystal, Matt, Jim, Sandy—many names just require you to be aware of the visual component. Some names require a little more imagination and effort.
  - An image for Bill could be a duck bill or a dollar bill.
  - An image for Joe could be a cup of coffee, or G.I. Joe.
  - An image for Tom could be a turkey or a cat.

It takes a little time to really get automatic with turning names into images, but most of our clients are surprised at how easy and fun it can be.

There are literally an infinite number of places to apply the mental file folder system and your brain's natural ability to visualize. Experiment with the techniques on your own, and feel free to reach out to us at Freedom Personal Development with specific questions.

Let's get to work on your other learning foundation: your Smart Reading capability!

**Reinforcement and Bonuses:** This chapter has been Memory Optimized™ for your benefit. For your brief lesson and some great bonuses, visit www.planetfreedom .com/trainyourbrain with the access code on page 232. Enjoy!

# Learning Foundation #2
# Your Smart Reading Capacity

*Special thanks in this section go to Abby Marks-Beale, author of *10 Days to Faster Reading, The Complete Idiot's Guide to Speed Reading*, and the RevItUp Reading Online Course. As America's premier authority on adult reading effectiveness, our trainers at Freedom Personal Development and I are deeply grateful for the mentorship and training Abby has given us.

# 4

# Why You Read Like a Sixth-Grader and What to Do about It

Your second learning foundation is your ability to read smarter. Remember RIF—Reading Is Fundamental? Reading is in fact a fundamental skill for life that is heavily emphasized throughout elementary school, with good reason. Everybody knows that kids who can't read well have a much higher likelihood of failure in school and in life.

So how would you describe yourself as a reader? Seriously, fill in the blank below.

I am a _____ reader.

The most common answers are pretty subjective. In our workshops the most common answers sound like:

- Fast
- Slow
- Good
- Bad

- Average
- Casual

Subjective terms. I want you to really think about your answer, because guess what? Right now, as a businessperson, a manager, a leader, a parent, or just as a grown-up, your ability to read effectively is actually *more* important for your success than it was back in elementary school. As a reader of this book, you likely are part of the information business. You generate your income with your mind more than with your hands. You're brains over brawn. That means that learning—not just keeping up but keeping ahead—is the fundamental competitive advantage that you have. Add to that the fact that the sheer volume of information that you, your competition, your customers, your colleagues, and your kids have access to and it becomes obvious that whatever your job is, a big part of that job is reading!

Which is why my next statement is problematic for you:
*In all likelihood, you read like a sixth-grader.*

That's right, you heard me. If you're like 99 percent of our clients, you're reading this book right now the exact same way you read books when you were in sixth grade. You're using the same technique, going the same speed, and comprehending the same percentage of what you read as you did when you were 11 years old.

This is not your fault. You aren't bad or lazy, you just haven't received any training in how to use your reading tools for a long time. Specifically, since about when? You got it—sixth grade. For nearly everyone, your formalized training in how to take words from a printed page (or computer screen) starts in about kindergarten and ends in about sixth grade. You may have had "reading class" for a few years after that, but mostly that was just reading books and discussing them. A terrific thing to do, no doubt, but you weren't being taught how to read. Let's find out where that's gotten you.

# Baseline Test

Just like we did with your recall capacity, you're going to do a short exercise to evaluate your starting point. For this exercise you need a pen and something to time yourself with. Any kind of stopwatch will do. Set your stopwatch to zero, then go to the beginning of the article you see in the next section. It's called "The Very Best of All Time," an article from my blog a few years ago. Start your timer, then read the article just like you would read anything else. Don't try to make it a race, just read it like you're currently reading these words.

Ready, set, go.

## The Very Best of All Time

I had the privilege of watching the most dominant team in recent sports memory—possibly the most dominant team ever—play for the national championship. Women's basketball may not be the gigantic draw that the men's tournament is, but it's the arena of the University of Connecticut women's basketball team. From 2008 to 2010, they were 78–0. That's right, 78 games in a row, including two national championships. Their smallest margin of victory over that stretch was 12 points. It's the second-longest winning streak ever in college basketball, outdone only by John Wooden's UCLA team, which won 88 games in a row. UConn only trailed at all in one game—they're totally dominant.

When I have the chance to see that powerful a team in a championship scenario it's worth staying up. It was not disappointing.

UConn was playing Stanford. Stanford was the lone team in the past two years to even hold a lead over the Huskies. The Huskies were heavily favored to win their second consecutive national championship. Lots of hype—history in the making, and so on. So in the first half, UConn lays an egg. They score 12 points, tying their school record for lowest point production in 130 years. They play terribly, miss nearly every shot; they stink. At halftime they trail by 15 and everyone is stunned. The first five minutes of the second half are more of the same—ugly to watch, embarrassing for UConn. But somewhere in there, they turn it around, outscore Stanford 41 to 20 in the second half, and go on to win the championship 53–47. Amazing game.

Here are some lessons that I found helpful.

### #1. Even the Very Best of All Time Have Their Off Times

UConn was definitively the best women's basketball team ever; it couldn't have been clearer. But the scoreboard doesn't lie. So how could the best team ever be so pathetic in their biggest game ever? Answer: It just happens sometimes. It just goes to show that even that level of excellence has to deal with adversity. I believe that you are among the best of all time. You wouldn't be reading this if you weren't. If you're having an off week, day, quarter, whatever—don't spazz, it happens occasionally. Do what you can to:

### #2. Remember Who You Are

UConn clearly had forgotten who they were in the first half. They played like the least skilled, least confident, least motivated team in the country, which was clearly not who they were. I don't know what happened in the huddle (how cool would it be to hear that?), but something caused that group of women to remember that they were the very best. You do the same: Remember how fantastic you are. Replay your successes in your mind, even little ones. Look back on what you've done, victories you've achieved. Sometimes it's easy to forget the greatness that we each possess, and when we re-remember it, POW! You begin your comeback.

How long did it take you to read that? _____ minutes and _____ seconds

The article you just read is exactly 500 words, so you could determine your baseline reading speed by dividing 500 by your time, expressed as a decimal. Better yet, just use the chart shown in Figure 4.1.

Baseline reading speed: _____ WPM

| If your time was: | Your WPM was: |
|---|---|
| :10 | 3,125 |
| :20 | 1,515 |
| :30 | 1,000 |
| :40 | 750 |
| :50 | 600 |
| 1:00 | 500 |
| 1:10 | 470 |
| 1:20 | 375 |
| 1:30 | 333 |
| 1:40 | 300 |
| 1:50 | 272 |
| 2:00 | 250 |
| 2:10 | 230 |
| 2:20 | 215 |
| 2:30 | 200 |
| 2:40 | 187 |
| 2:50 | 177 |
| 3:00 | 167 |
| 3:10 | 158 |
| 3:20 | 150 |
| 3:30 | 143 |
| 3:40 | 136 |
| 3:50 | 130 |
| 4:00 | 125 |
| 4:10 | 120 |
| 4:20 | 115 |
| 4:30 | 111 |
| 4:40 | 107 |
| 4:50 | 103 |
| 5:00 | 100 |

**Figure 4.1**

## What Your Score Means

Here's what various speeds indicate about your reading. Please keep in mind that your score does not reflect your character or your intellect. A below-average reading speed doesn't make you a below-average human. It just means that you read slowly. The good news about all of this is that wherever you are starting from, you have the ability to improve dramatically. Look at the following to see how your score stacks up.

**A WPM of under 200 is below average**, and it means you're what we call a *talker*. Operating at this speed, you are essentially reading out loud to yourself. What I mean is that you are saying every word you're reading in your head. You may not notice it, but it's likely that when you read your lips move. The positive in this is that you're a very careful reader and you believe comprehension is way more important than speed. The downside of this is that reading takes you a long time, plus you're operating under an incorrect premise. Reading slowly does not necessarily increase comprehension—in fact, the opposite is usually true.

**A WPM of 200 to 300 is average**. It's average for adults, and it's average for sixth-graders. At that stage of your reading development, you had become effective at reading one word at a time. Reading one word at a time seems logical, but with the way your eyes actually operate while reading, the idea of reading only one word at a time will limit your speed. With a couple of other habits you probably have, it will also make your eyes and brain tired more quickly than opening up the throttle.

**A WPM of 300 to 450 is above average**, and it means a couple of things. It means that as a reader, you are what we call a *thinker*. You're not focused on hearing every word in your head, your eyes are moving a little faster, and you're probably thinking of concepts when you read. You're making connections and/or actively processing what you read. It also means that you probably do a lot of reading, either because you like to or you have to. Just through sheer practice volume, you move slightly faster than average. Congratulations.

Statistically, at least 90 percent of the readers of this book are starting in one of these three places, but just in case:

**Over 450 is considered "tuned-up."** Either consciously or unconsciously, you are doing something that allows you to take in more than one word at a time, and/or you may not be trying to read every single word. If you are in this range, congratulations! You're probably doing some of the things we'll teach in this section.

The best news is that no matter where you are starting from right now, you unquestionably have the ability to make massive improvements to both speed and comprehension pretty quickly.

I've done it myself. When Abby Marks-Beale tested me the first time, I was 38 years old, and I thought I was above average in reading speed. I like to read, I know the importance of reading, and I do it a lot. I was correct, I came in at 340 WPM, about as fast as an above-average sixth-grader. Just by learning how to use my eyes more rhythmically I immediately went to over 700, and a little practice brought me close to 1,000 WPM. Other techniques (taught in the next chapter) have taken and kept me even faster than that, with comprehension that's at least as good as it was at lower speeds.

Our students have done it all over the country. In our live workshops we've had middle-schoolers, high-schoolers, and college students go from 200 WPM to over 1,200 in the space of one day, with a significant increase in comprehension. I've seen adults from all walks of life get the same results with every conceivable kind of reading material.

The fastest readers in the world consistently read 5,000 to 10,000 words per minute, with near perfect comprehension. I know it sounds crazy, but the potential of the human mind is, in fact, astounding. Do you need to do 10,000 words per minute? Probably not. I mean, that level essentially represents a lifetime of practice like a Shaolin monk. But consider what it would mean for your effectiveness if you could just double your speed and keep your comprehension the same. More important, *consider the impact of being able to read however fast you want, at whatever level of comprehension you need, based on what's right for you in your particular situation.* Because that's what you can do quickly, with just a little training.

## The Concept of "Gears" in Smart Reading

It's helpful to understand the concept of "gears" when reading. There are times when you will want to be very methodical and very detailed. You're reading a report, a contract, or perhaps some material that is totally foreign to you, but you need to really get it for a test. Other times, you're reading for more general information, maybe in something where you already know a lot about the subject. There are times when slow is appropriate, others when the need for speed is there.

Grown-up reading means that you can adjust your speed in the way that works for you in the given situation. When driving a car, first gear is perfect for going 15 miles an hour past the school zone, but if you're out on the freeway, first gear will literally burn out your engine. Most people, starting around sixth grade, only operate in one gear ever—first. When you develop higher "reading gears," you give yourself choices you didn't have before.

## Three Reading Habits You Can Reduce

To develop those higher gears, you first need to be aware of what's holding you back. If you know how to read at all, there are three things that you habitually do while reading. You may not know you do them, but you do. Reducing any or all of them will dramatically improve your focus, your speed, and your comprehension.

## Mind Wandering (aka Daydreaming)

Have you ever been reading, reached the end of a page or chapter, and realized you had zero clue as to what you just read? That's because your mind wandered away. It's weird—your eyes actually traveled over the page, but your brain was occupied with—who knows? Point is, you had literally zero comprehension of what you read, and you then had to start all over again!

Now there is actually a place and time where this habit is useful. When what you're reading causes your mind to make a connection and wander to something related to your reading material, that's actually very helpful. Daydreaming is totally unhelpful when your mind is just, well, wandering.

*The basic fix for this habit is simple—go faster!* Your mind wanders largely because it's bored. If it has the ability to easily take in, say, double what you're currently doing (it does), your brain just has too much extra capacity and it will use it for something else. When you challenge your brain with more speed, your brain loves it and stays more engaged. This will dramatically boost comprehension.

## Regression (aka Going Back)

Nearly everyone, while reading anything, will regularly go back and reread what they just read. If you watch their eyes, you can actually see it happening. Most of the time we don't even know we're doing it! As you can imagine, this process of regression slows you down dramatically, and it's usually not necessary.

Again, there is a time and a place for this habit. If you go back in your reading purposefully looking for something you missed, then regression will assist your learning. Usually however, regression is a result of either your mind wandering or just habit. In these cases, you're unnecessarily doubling the amount of time you're spending.

The best way we've found to reduce this habit is to *cut off your escape route*. One of the techniques taught in Chapter 5 does this brilliantly and will pretty much eliminate unwanted regression.

### Subvocalization (aka Mental Whispering)

The last habit you probably want to reduce is called subvocalization—the attempt to hear every word in your head. If you're doing this, you limit your reading speed to no more than your speaking speed, which is only about 150 WPM.

Subvocalization is actually wonderful when you're reading a form of literature where the hearing of words is integral to the experience. Some material is written expressly to hear it—scripture, dialogue, and poetry fall into this category. Outside of that, subvocalization serves no purpose other than to slow you down and make you work a lot harder than you need to.

The best way to reduce this habit (actually, all three habits) is to use your eyes and/or hands (your Smart Reading tools), more actively and mindfully, learning to engage the visual centers of your brain in favor of the auditory centers. This is the essence of what you'll learn next.

**Reinforcement and Bonuses:** This chapter has been Memory Optimized™ for your benefit. For your brief lesson and some great bonuses, visit www.planetfreedom .com/trainyourbrain with the access code on page 232. Enjoy!

# 5

# Your Smart Reading Tools for Improved Focus and Speed

I f you want to improve your focus, your speed, your comprehension (or all three), what do you *do*? This chapter will give you a little theory; more important, it will help you understand the tools you have at your disposal, then teach you the most effective and efficient way of using them.

## The Mechanics of the Reading Process

At its base level, "reading" simply means "to look at and understand symbols." It's important to understand that if you are not understanding, you are not reading. There is a difference between "speed reading" and "speed looking." You have two innate tools that are necessary for reading, and one that can be helpful, but isn't necessary. Your *eyes* and your *brain are* necessary for reading—inherently, reading is a visual process. Your *hands* or other tools are not necessary, but when used properly, your hands and other tools can be extremely helpful for enhancing your focus and overall engagement.

One big key to understand is that your mouth is usually profoundly unhelpful, since it slows you down. Again, except for the circumstances listed previously (poetry, dialogue, or scripture), reading should engage the visual centers of the brain, which as you've seen are extremely fast. Mouth reading (subvocalization) engages the auditory centers, which are much slower. As much as possible, leaving that auditory part of your brain out of your reading will make your process much smoother and more efficient. It can take some conscious effort to let go of this habit, but it's worth it.

Ultimately, you will choose to read faster with your brain. The brain is ultimately what decides how much it will allow in. However, training your eyes is always the correct place to start, as nearly everyone uses their eyes in an undisciplined manner.

## Understanding Your Eyes

When you read, your eyes *jump*. Specifically, they jump four times per second; if you watch it, it's pretty amazing (and a little freaky). In our live workshops, we have people pair up and read some text with a partner watching their eyes. What's amazing is that from an outside perspective you can actually see what people do with their eyes when they read. The most frequent word that people use to describe how it looks is "typewriter." Try it out sometime. If you can find a willing partner, watch them read some text and you'll see their eyes hop from word to word, left to right, then go back to the left, like a typewriter. If you watch long enough, you'll also see their eyes regress, either back to the left or even back up the page (for a full visual of what

I'm describing, check out the bonus video listed at the end of this chapter).

The only people you won't see this typewriter action with are people who read more than 500 words per minute (WPM) approximately. With people who read at that speed, you'll see that their eye movements are much smoother and more fluid. It's quite remarkable, and here's why this is important.

### *Two Eye-Movement Terms You Should Understand*

**Fixation:** When reading, your eye muscles will cause your eyes to stop four times per second. Each stop is called a *fixation*. When your eyes are stopped is the only time that information can register through to your brain. While moving between jumps, the eyes are moving so fast that nothing gets in. So while you're reading, information is entering through your eyes four times per second. This is largely a biological process, not one that can be trained. It's just how eye muscles work. You can't really influence how often your eyes stop. What you can influence is how many words you let in at each stop.

**Eye Span:** Your *eye span* is the width of text that your eyes take in every time your eyes stop. Most people read with the narrowest possible eye span: one word per stop. The math ads up, too: if you read one word per fixation, that's four words per second. That's exactly 240 words per minute—average sixth-grade reading speed! The nuts and bolts of increasing reading speed is simply to widen your eye span and take in more words at each stop. It's just like if you're trying to walk across a field, being locked into taking four steps per second. If you take little steps, you'll take a long time to get across the field. Longer strides at the same rate get you there much faster and with less effort.

Widening your eye span is actually quite easy to do. It just takes a little training of the eye muscles, and a little practice.

### Improving Your Eye Function

Let's start with the muscles that move your eyes.

Do this exercise:

Stand up straight and look straight ahead. Without moving your head, look as far to your left as you can. Then look as far to your right as possible. Then go back and forth on a level plane with your eyes five times as fast as you can. Now sit down.

Did that make you dizzy or hurt your eyes? It does for most people, and that means you have poorly trained, weak eye muscles. To strengthen and condition those muscles, try doing the exercise you just did a couple of times a day. You'll notice very quickly (even after just one or two days in most cases) that this exercise becomes much less taxing as your eye muscles strengthen.

Here's how to get your eyes to move in a more rhythmic manner when you read. The idea is that you want to be able to feel your eyes kind of bouncing along the page. Here's an exercise that we do in our live workshops. Read the following page, then read it again, following the instructions given.

**Discipline Your Eyes Exercise**

The purpose   of this page   is to discipline
the little muscles   that move the eyes   from left to right.
Incorrect habits   of reading   have frequently caused
these muscles   to behave   in an undisciplined
and inefficient manner.   Try to make   your eyes march ahead
in three   rhythmic leaps   across the line.
Try to feel   the tiny tug   on these six
little muscles   that move each eye.   You will note
that some phrases   are short   others are longer.
This is done   intentionally.   The amount
of line width   that various people   can see differs
with the individual.   In these exercises   try to group
as one eyeful   all the words   in the unit;
look at a point   just about midway   in each word group.
At times   you will feel   as though the field
of your vision   is being stretched.   So much the better!
At other times   the phrase will be too short.
We shall strive   for wider and wider   units as we proceed.
In that way   your eyes will grasp   more and more
at a glance.   Read this exercise   two or three times
every day   for a few days.   Try always
to cut down   on the time   that it took you
to read it   each preceding time.   You will soon get
the knack of it.   Do not let   your eyes "skid"
or "slide"   when you look   at a phrase.
Look at it   in the middle.   Give it a strong,
fleeting glance.   See it all   in one look;
then be off   to see the next   and the next,
and so on   to the very end   of the exercise.
And now,   how long   did it take you
to read this?   Mark your time   on the bottom of   this page.

How did that go? To train your eyes for rhythmic movement, read that page using your "eye bounce" a couple of times a
day. Don't worry about comprehension; the point of the exercise
is simply to train your eyes to move rhythmically. And time
yourself. If it took you longer than one minute, try and get it
below a minute. Keep working at it until you can get it under 30
seconds, then under 20, then under 15. At that rate, your eyes
would be moving at a 1,000+ WPM pace.

In fact, we recommend that you keep a copy of this page
(see the bonus section for a downloadable copy) everywhere you
read, and use it to groove those muscles before launching into
any reading session. Like a golfer on the putting green, you'll
serve your eyes well if you warm them up in this fashion before
reading anything. Fortunately, because the eye muscles are so
fast twitch, they respond to training very quickly. Practice the
eye exercises for a few days and you'll notice that your eyes don't
get tired nearly as fast.

## Using Your Hands Properly

Your second tool for boosting reading speed is your hands. As we
mentioned, it is not necessary to use your hands at all, but most
of our students find it very helpful. The reason why is twofold:

1. Using a hand technique (or pace card) makes reading more
   physically engaging. Fact is, you're less likely to fall asleep!
   As you learned in the memory section of *Train Your Brain*,
   the more active or physically engaged you are while learning, the better your learning turns out.

2. Your brain is hardwired to make your eyes notice motion.
   This dates back to our hunter/gatherer days, when motion
   indicated something that either wanted to eat you or you

wanted to eat. One inherent challenge with most reading material is that it doesn't move. This is why it's so easy to get distracted while reading. A bird flying by the window can do it, the TV will do it, just about anything that moves can attract your attention. Using a hand or card technique puts movement on the page you are reading, in a way that should enhance your focus and help your eyes move more rhythmically and quickly.

In our live workshops, there are 13 hand/card techniques we have our students experiment with. Here I'll give you the ones that we see used most often. Experiment with some until you find one that feels comfortable and enhances your focus.

The first category includes what I call the *finger pull* techniques. You use either your right or left index finger for this. Not a pen, not your knuckles, your index finger, aka your pointer. The idea of the finger pull techniques is that as you're reading, you pull that finger vertically down the page at a consistent pace that is just slightly faster than your eyes can keep up with. The idea is to keep that finger moving down the page consistently—no stopping and no going back up the page with it. You can try pulling your pointer down the left margin, the right margin, or the center of the column of text. Don't push so hard that you're fingertip turns white; just do a nice easy pull down the page. If you want to really engage your body, try what's called double pointer pull. That's where you're using both your right and left pointers at the same time, going down both right and left margins. Take a moment and try these out on any page of text in this book. See which one you like best.

Got your favorite finger pull technique? Great, now compare it to what we call the *pace card*. The pace card technique is far and away the most popular technique in our live workshops. To use it, all you need is a 3 by 5 index card, or even a blank piece of paper folded in half. Even a business card could work, though it might be a little small. The only rule on what to use as a pace card is that you need to be able to hold it easily with one hand.

Where you put your pace card in relation to what you're reading is the entire key. Take your pace card and place it *above the line you're reading*. That's right, I said *above the line*. "But wait a minute!" you say, "I can't see what I just read!" Exactly. The main reason this technique immediately boosts speed and focus in over 90 percent of our students is that it eliminates the possibility of regression, and your brain knows it. You've cut off your escape route, so your subconscious knows that it needs to pay attention, because it only has one chance. So as you're reading, just start moving the card down the page at a nice, comfortable, steady rate that keeps your eyes moving forward. Ideally the card doesn't stop, and it definitely doesn't go back up. Try the pace card technique on any page of this book for a minute or two and see how you like it.

Which one do you prefer? Finger or card? You're not locked in forever, but decide which one to try out, because you're going to do another quick test. Same as before: Time yourself reading the following article, this time using the hand/card technique you've chosen.

Ready, set, go!

# Find Your Smile

I was listening to a guy named Andy Andrews speak, and he said something that hit me right between the eyes. Mr. Andrews said that if he only got one minute on stage and one thing to say that would change someone's life, it would be easy. He said his advice would be to:

*Smile while you talk.*

That's it—crazy, huh? So simple, but so true. In coaching our clients on communications, I see so many places where someone is succeeding, and you can hear them smiling while they're talking. In person or on the phone, you really can hear it! On the other hand, I've listened to people struggling, and you can usually hear them frowning while talking. Smile while you talk—if there's a magical sales bullet, that's it.

So I always get asked "How do you do this?" Fair question. My initial answer was "use a mirror," which is a good physical step, especially on the phone. My friend Eric Plantenberg's answer was deeper: He said "live a life of gratitude." A forced smile is sometimes better than no smile, but clearly the all-time winner is a sincere smile that comes from within. Brian Tracy says that "the most powerful thing a salesperson can do is to walk into a meeting with a smile just leaving their lips."

Sometimes finding that true smile is harder to do than others—okay. My core value of joy is exemplified by the ability to find our smile even when the poop hits the fan. Two methods that seem to work every time are:

*Honest communication with a coach.* Really letting someone know what's going on inside is incredibly liberating. I've had hundreds of these pressure-valve type of talks where both of us felt lighter after the talk, and both of us saw better results immediately. I'm not talking about just bitching to anyone who'll listen (one of the unhealthiest things you can do), but a proper airing of the soul with someone who can help.

*The gratitude list*—done as a part of everyday living. Practicing gratitude is helpful even done once, but it's amazing when we make it a habit. By really appreciating yourself, your life, and the people you interact with daily, you find your smile so fast and so strong it makes your head spin.

Find your smile and good things will find you.

Time to read: _____ min, _____ sec.

That article was exactly 400 words. Check the chart in Figure 5.1 for the WPM that corresponds with your time.

Faster this time? About 90 percent of our clients see at least some improvement even the first time they try a hand or card technique; for many, the improvement is dramatic. We've seen droves of people triple, even quadruple their reading speed with just the white card technique, practiced over a few weeks.

| If your time was: | Your WPM was: |
| --- | --- |
| :10 | 2,400 |
| :20 | 1,200 |
| :30 | 800 |
| :40 | 600 |
| :50 | 480 |
| 1:00 | 400 |
| 1:10 | 345 |
| 1:20 | 300 |
| 1:30 | 265 |
| 1:40 | 240 |
| 1:50 | 220 |
| 2:00 | 200 |
| 2:10 | 200 |
| 2:20 | 170 |
| 2:30 | 160 |
| 2:40 | 150 |
| 2:50 | 140 |
| 3:00 | 135 |
| 3:10 | 125 |
| 3:20 | 120 |
| 3:30 | 115 |
| 3:40 | 110 |
| 3:50 | 105 |
| 4:00 | 100 |

Figure 5.1

It is possible that your speed stayed the same, or possibly even decreased. That would be due to the fact that *it was your first time doing this*. Due to that newness, sometimes the mind focuses on "Am I doing this right?" versus just doing it. If that was you, try it again and relax—you don't need to be perfect. Keep experimenting until you find what works for you.

Whether you improved a little, a lot, or not at all, it bears repeating *that this was only your first time*. A little practice with any of these techniques can do wonders, especially when you combine them with the strategies for comprehension and retention found in Chapter 6.

Keep using the Discipline Your Eyes exercise regularly, and practice your hand or card technique with everything you read for the next couple of weeks, and you'll blow your mind at how much faster you'll get. Your comprehension will, in many cases, go up as your speed increases.

**Reinforcement and Bonuses:** This chapter has been Memory Optimized™ for your benefit. For your brief lesson and some great bonuses, visit www.planetfreedom .com/trainyourbrain with the access code on page 232. Enjoy!

# 6

# Your Smart Reading Tools for Enhanced Comprehension and Retention

Just reading faster is not the end all be all. If you don't understand what you're reading, you can whip your eyes along at a million miles an hour and it won't do you much good. In this chapter, you'll learn one concept, three questions, and one awesome technique for prepping your brain to combine speed with comprehension. You'll also learn how to actively process what you read so that you retain it at the highest level possible.

## The Balance

First off, let's clear up a myth: *reading faster does not hurt your comprehension*. Many of our students struggle with the misconception that if they read faster, they won't understand what they're reading. I understand how it feels this way, and there are times when you do want to be methodical in your approach. Remember the concept of gears? In specific instances where you are reading material that is very heavy, perhaps very technical, or about something that you have little background knowledge of, then a slower pace can be very helpful. But the blanket assumption that faster always means less gets in is false. In fact, the opposite is true: Comprehension increases with speed.

That may seem counterintuitive, but it makes sense if you just think about it for a moment. Most of your sixth-grade lack of speed is due to the three habits we discussed in Chapter 4:

- Mind Wandering
- Regression
- Subvocalization

Reducing these three is proven to improve speed, and a lot of that increase comes from the dramatic increase in focus required to counteract those habits. You cannot use eye discipline or any hand or card technique mindlessly; you must be *conscious*.

Doesn't it stand to reason that the same increased focus that boosted your speed should also help your comprehension? This is borne out in our workshops, where it's very common for our students to see comprehension and speed rise together, up to a point. True, sometimes comprehension dips a little *at first*. This is because the new technique is a little uncomfortable at first, so sometimes your brain gets a little thrown off.

Notice, however, that I said speed and comprehension rise together up to a point. Wherever you are in your progress, there is that line between reading and just looking. Your job is to find where that line is for you, and keep pushing it up. What we know is true, however, is that the increase in speed always *precedes* the increase in comprehension. So in improving your overall effectiveness as a reader, you'll be well served to temporarily let go of comprehension. Focus on speed first, let your comprehension catch up, and settle in at a higher level; then repeat that cycle.

To set yourself up for success, here are three smart questions to ask yourself before you read anything.

1. **Why am I reading this?**
2. **What do I need this information for?**
3. **How much time do I have?**

Asking these three questions before you read anything is powerful. The answers are nothing to get hung up on—it's the questions themselves that will supercharge your overall effectiveness. By asking these questions, you just engage your brain in a way that it's ready to go—it's warmed up! These questions also add focus and context to what you're reading. When you add focus and context to anything, you will definitely perform better. Most importantly, they will prime your reticular activating system (RAS). Remember that part of your brain that makes you see the car you decided to buy? Asking yourself these questions is actually asking your brain, "What am I looking for here?" As we know from the introduction to this book, you will see what you look for, even on a level as micro as reading material.

If the only thing you did differently with reading was to ask these questions before diving into what you read, you would have a major impact on your reading effectiveness. The real beauty is that it takes about 10 seconds to ask the questions—10 seconds really well invested.

## Why and How to "Smart Read"

The single biggest thing that will quantum leap your reading speed and comprehension is *background knowledge*. If you have a lot of background knowledge of what you're reading, your brain will naturally predict what's going to be said next. This allows you to fill in the gaps accurately even when moving at a high rate of speed. Background knowledge also allows you to instinctively know when you can just skim over a section or when you should really dig in, maybe even take some notes. Background knowledge is the nuclear bomb for boosting comprehension and speed together. Nothing is more powerful.

So how do you gain background knowledge about a new piece of reading material if you don't already have it? Learn to Smart Read!

Smart Reading (formerly known as "cheat reading") is a simple process of deliberately *overviewing* a piece of reading material before *reading* it. You can Smart Read any piece of nonfiction—a book like this one, a newspaper, a magazine—anything that is not a story or a work of fiction. Here's why:

Every work of nonfiction is started with a *writer's outline*. The writer's outline is essentially the skeleton of the work. The writer creates the outline of main ideas first, then fleshes it out to make it interesting. *The main ideas of any work of nonfiction are found in the outline*. If you could read the writer's outline before you read the whole chapter/article/whatever, you'd develop a ton of background knowledge about that work. You'd literally find the road map, and you'd do it in very short order.

The good news is that you can read the outline first—it's just a little hidden! To overview a chapter or article, try this three-step process:

**Step 1**. Read the first paragraph. This is where you'll learn the overarching theme or purpose of the piece.

**Step 2**. Read the last paragraph. This usually ties the piece together or moves you on to what's next.

**Step 3**. Read the first sentence or two of each paragraph in between. This is where the main idea of that paragraph will be found. If you really want to be sure, you can also read the last sentence of the paragraph as a tie-down.

That's Smart Reading in a nutshell. You'll be blown away by how much you can prime your mind for what you read by doing a Smart Read first. Here are the three best ways to use Smart Reading:

1. *As a weeding tool*. Often the overview will teach you everything you want or need to know. Maybe you actually know

more than the author does, maybe you just don't need the information right now; maybe you don't need it ever. In that case you can just skip the whole thing before you even get started. What a relief!

2. *As an overview.* Assuming that you do want to continue after your Smart Read overview, you now know all the main ideas you'll be learning. You've jacked up your background knowledge and gotten your brain ready to absorb at a very high level.

3. *As a review.* Even after you've read something, you may want to go back to it and review or refresh your memory. Maybe you're prepping for a test, maybe you want to fold the material into a presentation, and so on. A quick overview is just the ticket to bring it back to your mind.

So when you add up what you've learned in this section, you've got a very powerful way of both priming your brain to see what you need it to see and then giving it the road map for what you're about to read. When you combine the three Reading Smart questions with a Smart Read overview of your reading material, you'll be amazed at just how quickly you can digest information, with the highest levels of comprehension.

If you haven't done so already, I'd recommend that before each subsequent chapter in *Train Your Brain For Success* you ask the questions and then Smart Read it before diving in. You'll absorb more and internalize more quickly.

## The Key to Retention: Interactive Processing

The final issue we're going to work on in this section is the issue of *retention*. Have you ever read a book, thought "that was awesome," and then by a day or two later you couldn't remember what the book actually said? That's very natural, it happens to everyone, especially if you're reading unconsciously. There's a

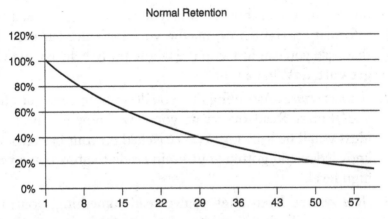

**Figure 6.1** The Ebbinghaus Forgetting Curve

fairly well known chart called the Ebbinghaus Forgetting Curve. You can find numerous versions of it, but it looks like the graph in Figure 6.1.

It basically shows how without review, recall of anything fades over time. This is why the spaced repetition concept (one hour, one day, one week) is so important for long-term retention.

As it applies to reading material, retention tends to fade even faster than life events or things learned more interactively. With unconscious reading (passive, word by word, no eye discipline, and no hand/card technique), you'll only retain about 10 percent of what you read after three days. Not the desired result. Fortunately, there are some fairly easy things you can do while reading to boost your retention to over 50 percent, even 75 percent. The key to all of them is that they make reading more interactive and involving. The more centers of your brain you can involve in processing what you read, the more you will retain.

## Retention Booster #1—Tuned-Up Reading

Simply doing what you've been learning to do in these last few chapters clearly makes the reading process more active and engaging. Using eye discipline, engaging your hands, using the three questions, and Smart Reading do so much to ramp up your focus that they have a powerful impact on your retention. Simply tuning up your reading in these ways can boost three-day retention to around 50 percent. That's significant.

### Retention Booster #2—Effective Highlighting

Effective highlighting while you read is another terrific strategy for retaining more. What's effective highlighting? If you've ever been reading and highlighted a whole page, that isn't it. That's not bad (it does help you pick out where you might want to spend more time the second time reading something), but it doesn't really do much for retention. Effective highlighting looks like what you see in this paragraph. You may be noticing that if you read a paragraph that looks like this, the writer's outline discussed earlier pops right out. Effective highlighting is selective, it requires conscious thought, and most of it will be in the beginning and end of a paragraph. This is another strategy that can boost your three-day retention to around 50 percent.

### Retention Booster #3—Margin Notes

*Margin notes* is a simple concept that you may already employ. This is when you read with a pen in your hand and make notes to yourself in the margin of the reading material itself. This is the next level of engagement, as it requires you to think, make connections, and process through your brain and then out your hand. Making margin notes is yet another technique that can take your retention to over 50 percent.

### Retention Blaster—Full Notes

If you want heavy-duty, armor-clad, lockdown hardcore retention, you want to go with *full notes*. "Full notes" is where you literally read with notetaking materials next to your reading material. As you read, you take short breaks to paraphrase what you're reading. You let the reading into your mind, process it, then explain it to yourself on paper in your own words. You can write down key words, mental connections to other works, bullet points, whole sentences—whatever works for you. The key to full notes is that you are totally making the material your own, with your mind, your eyes, your hands, and a pen. For a highly structured way of doing this, you can get or create a Cornell Notes notebook, with specially ruled pages and instructions in that method (worth checking out). Even with just regular notebooks, however, taking full notes skyrockets retention to around 75 percent.

Way to go! You've got some great tools and strategies for not only reading faster, but with better comprehension, focus, and retention of what you read. You're well-armed for the next leg of the *Train Your Brain* journey: creating your record-breaking performance!

**Reinforcement and Bonuses:** This chapter has been Memory Optimized™ for your benefit. For your brief lesson and some great bonuses, visit www.planetfreedom .com/trainyourbrain with the access code on page 232. Enjoy!

# Section 2

## The Components of Your Record-Breaking Life

# Component #1
# Having Energizing Goals

# 7

# Five Characteristics of an Energizing Goal

It seems like every personal development book or guru talks about the importance of goals. So let's clarify, and talk about what goals are actually for. It's my belief that goals for business, health, relationships, money, or family are there to give you three things, and three things only. Those three things are:

1. **Focus**
2. **Direction**
3. **A sense of urgency**

That's it—that's all you need. Think about a time in your life when you had those three things in abundance; maybe when you were really locked in on hitting a sales goal or completing a project you were totally jazzed about. Maybe you were planning a wedding. Maybe you were training for a marathon or some other big athletic event. Anytime you had something that you were totally fired up about, especially if there was some type of deadline involved, you had a high degree of focus, direction, and urgency, didn't you? If you can picture that time, how did you feel during that time? My guess is that you felt energized, happy, maybe couldn't wait to get out of bed and get going each day—yes? Well guess what—when your goals are structured in the way we'll do it, they can provide that same energy and joy for you now. They aren't there to to be used as a weapon or a star to wish upon; they are there to give you focus, direction, and a sense of urgency. Let's break these down.

# Focus

In order to function optimally, your brain must have a clear focus. Why is this so important? There are a couple of reasons.

## Focus Quiets Your Mind

If you've ever been around a young child that is upset, you may know that the first thing to do is check if the child is hungry or wet or overly tired, and if it's not one of those things, you can assume that the child is simply freaking out. And when you give a young child something to focus on—a set of keys, a toy, your face—something they can latch onto and pay attention to, it calms their mind. The same is true for us. Yes, our subconscious mind has many of the same traits as an infant. When we have a clear picture to focus on, a goal that we are moving toward, our minds become much calmer. Most of our minds are prone to some fairly unhelpful habits: overanalyzing, worrying, imagining the worst, or just racing a million miles an hour. Providing your mind and your life with a clear picture to focus on will do wonders for your energy and productivity in the here and now.

## Focus Turns on the Law of Attraction

A crystal clear mental focus is the thing that activates your subconscious mind to start seeking out and attracting the things you really desire. The only other option is playing the "negative attraction" trick on yourself.

My friend Dave was teaching his daughter Hana how to ride her bike without training wheels. She was just starting to get it, so Dave ran up the road ahead of her and said "You're doing great—*now don't run into the telephone pole!*" You know that a bike will pretty much go wherever you look, right? So of course, as soon as Dave told her what not to run into, that's where she looked, and just naturally ran straight into the obstacle. They repeated this until Dave made a small change. When he ran up the road and said, "You're doing great, Hana—now *ride straight toward me!*" she had no problem at all.

So the real deal with focus is that *your subconscious mind is going to focus on something*. We can't control the fact that it will find a focus. What we do have influence over is what it will find to focus on. If we give it nothing, its tendency will be to find something negative; that's just what the mind does. Then the next thing the subconscious does is to move powerfully toward its focus—without any questions. It's like a heat-seeking missile toward whatever picture it's seeing. By consciously providing your mind with a clear and positive focus, it turns that missile toward what you really want, rather than just what it finds by default.

## Direction

We've learned that human beings operate best when they know where they are going, and that the destination is one they have decided upon themselves. Think about anytime you went on a road trip or vacation. One of the most exciting parts was right at the beginning, yes? As soon as you started moving, you got a lift just from knowing that you were heading toward something fun. Even though you weren't anywhere close yet, you got the buzz right away. Same thing is true in life. Example: If you've ever had to get out of debt, think about when you started getting excited about doing it. Most of my clients who've ever had to do this tell me that it's not when the last dollar gets paid off, it's when the first dollar gets paid off that the momentum starts to build and the excitement and motivation kick in. Same thing goes for an exercise plan. You usually start reaping the motivation and self-esteem benefits long before you start seeing significant results; you reap them *as soon as you start moving* in the direction of your goals. Earl Nightingale actually defined success as "the progressive realization of a worthwhile goal." So in many ways, success itself, energy and enthusiasm, are all about simply having direction. Effectively structured goals will give you that direction, and they'll do it quickly.

## Sense of Urgency

What is a sense of urgency? A sense of urgency means that you are moving quickly and with purpose. Have you ever woken up in the morning and you were just moving and grooving? Not rushing around, but you had a lot to do, you were excited about it, and you just needed to get going? Think about how you moved. You didn't linger over the newspaper or just stand in the shower till the hot water ran out—you were moving with purpose. Or think about when you were getting packed at the last minute to go on a vacation you were really excited about. Same feeling—not crashing around recklessly, but doing what needed to be done, quickly, efficiently, and without wasted time.

Well-structured goals will give you the same feeling. When you have a clear target in mind and you are focused on it, you derive a level of excitement and urgency that can't be found in a life lived by accident.

To sum up, your mind works like a GPS. I got reminded of this recently when I had to make a trip to central Wisconsin for a speaking engagement. The client was a bank, our meeting was happening in a small town, and I had to drive about 90 miles of two-lane highways to get there. To make it tougher, most of the way that morning was enshrouded in very thick fog. So I told my GPS the address I needed to get to. I said "Find 140 Huron street, Berlin, Wisconsin." And my faithful Droid assessed where I was, located my destination, and literally drew a line right to where I needed to go. Neat!

Here's the key though: What did I need to give my GPS? That's right, I needed to give it exact, specific information on where I wanted to go.

What if I had said to my GPS, "Find bank"? What would have happened? My GPS would have basically just gone, "Huh?" It does a great job with specifics, but generalities return nothing but more questions. We've learned that your subconscious mind is almost exactly the same: If you give it very specific directions it does an amazing job of getting you there, but generalities it just doesn't know what to do with, so it tends to do nothing. Having clear cut, effectively structured goals is like providing your internal GPS with the specific directions that it needs.

So what creates an effectively structured goal? How do you create targets that will give you the focus, direction, and urgency that you need to overcome the adversities that you face? There are five characteristics that we've found make up a truly energizing goal.

1. An energizing goal must be *meaningful to you*. This may seem obvious, but most people skip right over it.

2. An energizing goal must be *specific* and *measurable*, and a deadline can really help. This is the part that I think most people tend to shy away from when setting goals. In live workshops I'll often ask my students to do the exercise that I had you do at the beginning of this book: Write down their most important goal. And do you know what? About 95 percent of what people write down is completely lacking in this trait. I see people write down things like "lose some weight," "make more money," "grow sales," I actually had one person write down "Be Awesome," Now these are what I would consider to be a good start, but they

lack the power we find in specificity. Go back to the GPS example from earlier. Your brain wants and craves a clear, focused picture of where you want it to take you. When it has that, it gets really fired up and gets to work immediately, in ways we sometimes can't even understand. When it doesn't have a clear picture it goes nowhere because all it knows is to try and stay safe, right where it is. Why do we do this to ourselves? Why do so many people resist the idea of a specific, measurable goal with a due date? Three words: fear of failure. When you say "I want more money," you have wiggle room. You can always escape with "Yeah, someday I'll have more money." You can procrastinate. I understand this not wanting to put it out there specifically, I really do. So you have a choice—you can either get specific in your intention and make something happen, or you can keep general and stay exactly where you are right now. The results are very predictable.

By giving your goals specific numbers, measurements, and deadlines you also create accountability, either internal or external. Accountability is yet another extremely powerful success accelerator, what most of us resist. All I can say is that accountability may the best and fastest way to get things done. When you accept accountability, you accept responsibility, and it is nearly impossible to make progress until you do this. Make your goals specific, and just observe how much more they do for you.

3. An energizing goal must be the *right size*. How big should your goals be? For your goals to work, they will need to be the right size. What is the right size for you? Two elements are important.

First, the goals must be small enough that you genuinely believe you can accomplish them. There is a psychological term called "gradient" that applies here. Essentially we all have a limit on what we believe is possible for us. If a goal or objective is too far above that gradient, our brains simply don't consider it real or possible, and they will tend to give up before we even start. So if you are looking to increase your sales by 500 percent from one year to the next when you're accustomed to increasing by 10 to 20 percent, you may be simply making too much of a jump for your brain to handle.

Second, the goals must be big enough to make you stretch; they must make you a little uncomfortable. At the same time, you'll benefit a lot if you make your goals big enough that they will test you. Sure, achievable and realistic are important, but your brain loves a challenge! If you've run a marathon, your brain can't get very excited about your goal to run a 10K. Plus, setting and going for goals that are just out of easy reach is how you stretch yourself and grow as a person.

How can you tell if your goal is the right size for you? If your goal is the right size, it will create two distinct emotional responses. The first is that when you look at your goal in its totality, it should make you a little nervous. Not totally freak you out, but it should make the heart beat a little faster, maybe make your palms sweat a little. The second response is: When you break down the specific daily or weekly action steps toward your goal's achievement, it should instill confidence. You should be able to look at your goal in small pieces and say, "Oh yeah, I can do that." If you've got that combination of emotions, you can rest assured that you've got something that is at least the right size for you.

4. An energizing goal must be *written down* and ideally *turned into images*. I know, you've heard this one before: I need to write down my goals, blah blah blah. For some reason people tend to pooh-pooh this one, but if you're serious about accomplishing your goals, writing down your goals is not just a good idea that everyone talks about; it is one of the central elements that define an effectively structured goal. In speaking and conducting workshops on goals for more than a decade, I have found that nearly everyone pays lip service to this practice, but almost nobody does it on a regular basis. And it's crazy!

Napoleon Hill, in his incredible work *Think and Grow Rich*, describes a very specific process of identifying your "Definite

Chief Aim" and then writing about it in a very specific way. I won't detail it here, but it's fantastically effective, and Hill says that the technique and the thinking behind it were so effective for him and his students that it "frightened him." Read the book if you haven't, but he's basically talking about how the writing and reading of goals is one of the most powerful things one can do.

Here's a more modern example. A few years ago I hired a salesperson who was also a very successful competitive body builder. The discipline required to morph his body into a contest-winning work of art was staggering. But he did it—trained systematically and religiously, ate nothing but protein and vegetables for months on end, and regularly won bodybuilding contests. At the same time, he was failing miserably in sales. One day in a coaching session our conversation turned to his goals. I asked, "If I wanted to see your bodybuilding goals, where could I see them?" He said, "Oh, all over the place—my locker, my car, my apartment. I've got a whole notebook where they're written out and I've even got all kinds of pictures posted. Just talking about them right now is getting me all fired up!" I said, "Great, I love it. So if I wanted to see your sales goals, where could I see them?" And it was like I had punched him in the face. He was stunned, and slowly said, "You would have to look deep within the recesses of my brain." Hmmm...written out goals and tremendous success in one area, no written goals and no success in another. Correlation?

Where should goals be written? There's no pat answer but here are some suggestions. I use a notebook that I review daily. Also, written notes in places you'll see them are very helpful. On the fridge, in front of your desk at work, in your car, on the back of your computer—basically anywhere you can post your goals so that they act as a constant subconscious reminder can be extremely powerful. One thing that's very popular these days is the concept of a vision board/vision book, which takes the process to a whole other level. Keep in mind that your subconscious mind thinks in pictures. If you can create an image of success for your mind to focus on in conjunction with a written description, it's even better.

5. An effective goal must be *reviewed*. I always encourage my students to develop a relationship with their goals. And by relationship, I mean just like a relationship with a person who's important. When you can relate to your goals in a way that they become part of you—internalized—then their achievement is virtually assured. A mentor of mine once said, "I should be able to call you at two in the morning, wake you from a dead sleep, and ask you your most important goals, and you should be able to state them as quickly as if I had asked you your name."

Could you do that? Are you that clear and that well versed in the direction of your life? Most people are not, If you want to really develop focus, direction, and a sense of urgency through your goals you must spend time with them. You don't build a relationship with your spouse or your friends unless you spend time with them. You can't pass the 2 A.M. test if you've not internalized your goals, which doesn't happen at one sitting. You've got to review and re-view your goals. By "review," I mean go over your most important goals weekly by studying and measuring your progress; and by "re-view" I mean have the visual images that will continuously remind your subconscious of the picture you want it to be focused on. By doing this, you'll discover that you find more energy, meaning, context, and purpose in nearly everything you do, and positive things may begin to manifest in your world, almost like magic.

So those are the five main characteristics of an effectively structured goal. It will be *meaningful to you*; it will be *specific and measurable* with (potentially) a due date; it will be *the right size*; it will be *written down/visualized*; and it will be *re-viewed*. Here's the best thing about having goals structured in this way—even when it doesn't work, it still works!

Example: I remember the first time my business partner and I ever found ourselves in debt. Neither of us had really ever carried any debt, but we made some significant investments in our new business and found ourselves owing $47,000 at the beginning of a year. We were uncomfortable with the situation and set a goal of getting the entire amount paid off by my birthday, May 29. So we did all the things discussed here. We came up with exactly what we wanted to accomplish, gave ourselves the due date, and came up with every reason we could think of why it was important to us. We agreed that it would be a stretch but it was doable (right size), and we wrote all of this down. We even came up with signs with the number 4729 on them and posted them literally everywhere. It was actually a little ridiculous, but it worked. Good news is that our loan did not get paid off by May 29—it was actually paid on April 30. And I have to say, that result is very common. When you pick goals that are meaningful and then structure them in a way that really works, it's extremely common to achieve them faster than you ever thought possible. And even if it takes an extra week, month, or year, so what! If your goals are structured effectively, they will for sure provide you with focus, direction, and a sense of urgency that benefits you immediately, and that's worth the effort.

**Reinforcement and Bonuses:** This chapter has been Memory Optimized™ for your benefit. For your brief lesson and some great bonuses, visit www.planetfreedom .com/trainyourbrain with the access code on page 232. Enjoy!

# 8

# Heighten Your Focus with Your Keystone Goal

What we'll do now is to show you how to set up, tweak, and systemize your most important goals in a way that heightens your focus. There are five things I'm going to encourage you to do with your goals here, and I strongly encourage you to physically do the first three of them immediately. For this chapter you'll need a calendar, a clean sheet of paper, and a pen. Please make it pen and paper, not your computer screen. The things we are about to do are much more powerful when you do them by hand, so if you don't have pen and paper, go get some.

There are lots of ways to approach your goals, and I encourage you to explore lots of them. The approach we're going to take here is designed specifically to work within the parameters of what your brain can easily focus on. This is what I do with my own goals and it's what I have my coaching clients do with theirs. So this approach is not theory. It's not just some experiment that we cooked up. Believe me, I've done the experimenting myself! I've found that when I execute this particular method of approaching my goals, I accomplish what I aim for, usually faster than the time frame I give myself. If I ever find that I've missed a target, I can nearly always trace it back to how I didn't really do what you're about to do. This process is designed to give you a clear picture of what will be your most impactful goals to move toward right now. And if you do this right, strong positive motivation becomes a natural outgrowth of the process.

## Step 1—Narrow It Down

Write down the five or six most important things you want to accomplish in the next 90 days. Why five or six, and why 90 days? The key here at this stage is to *narrow it down*. Narrow the time frame, and narrow the number of items on the list. Why?

It's five or six goals because we've learned that your conscious mind simply doesn't deal well with too much information. It can only focus easily on a few things at a time. Now there is certainly a time and a place for what's called dream building, where you remove all limits on your thinking and on time and just go crazy thinking the biggest thoughts you can. That exercise is incredibly valuable for stretching your thinking and expanding your mind, which is not what we're doing here.

So get out a calendar and determine the next logical breakpoint that's about 90 days away. End of a quarter is ideal, and end of a month is fine, too. If your endpoint is 80 days or a hundred, that's fine; just make it about 90 days. Why is this important? That's about the amount of time that a human being can stay highly focused on one major objective without hitting the reset button and still see real progress.

Think about it; there's a reason why nearly every diet or exercise program is about 90 days in length. The wildly popular P90X fitness series is a great example. The P stands for Power and the X stands for Xtreme, which is mostly just marketing. But there's a ton of good science in the 90. The 90 stands for 90 days, and there's a pretty specific reason for this. It isn't P10X because you just can't see much progress in 10 days. At the same time it's not P300X because nobody can stay on track for that long all at one stretch. Why do you think that Wall Street places such high importance on quarterly financial reports for companies? Because that's about the right amount of time for an organization to make significant changes without losing focus. For anything significant, much less than 90 days is just too short to see any real progress, and much more than 90 is just too far out to see clearly.

Look at the next 90 days, and then number your paper 1 to 6. Not 7 or 10—just 6. You are going to write down the five or six most important goals you want to reach in that 90-day time frame. Now consider all the areas of your life—professional, financial, physical health, mental/emotional, family, and community—and make your list somewhat well rounded. Again, narrow it down; that's the key here. Anyone watching this likely has lots of things they want to accomplish. I'm guessing about you that you probably tend to try to do too much rather than too little, so you'll most likely benefit from allowing yourself no more than six spots to fill. It's totally okay if you can only come up with five, but do yourself a favor—limit yourself to a maximum of six items.

Now as you're writing out the handful of most important goals over the next 90 days, let's just review what makes a goal effective. In the last chapter we spent time on five characteristics that should be present in your goals, but I'll review them briefly here as well.

1. What you're writing should be *meaningful to you*. These objectives are no one's but yours, so make sure you get down what you really want to accomplish.

2. What you're writing should be *specific and measurable*. We're talking about a 90-day program with a very clear end point, so don't just write down "boost income," "lose weight," or "save some money." Be clear with yourself: What are

you specifically intending to accomplish between now and 90 days from now? Specifically, how much money do you intend to make or save? Specifically, How much weight do you intend to take off? Specifically, how many miles will you run? Specifically, how much will you sell? I do not care what the numbers or the specifics are, but it is critically important that you make it specific. If you neglect this, you miss out on most of the power in this process.

3. What you're writing does need to be *the right size* for you—big enough to be a challenge for you, but small enough that you genuinely believe you can accomplish it. Keep in mind, you've only got about three months for this before hitting the reset button. So size the goals appropriately. In doing this exercise, you may have to make a choice between "Should I think a little too big and stretch myself?" versus "Should I err on the side of safety?" How you handle that depends on your experience and your track record. If you are accustomed to automatically hitting your most important goals or if you're just a little bored, then go big. If you're doing this for the first time, then I would maybe err on the side of smaller.

4. This may go without saying, but what you are writing needs to be *written down*. Seriously, don't do you or me the disservice of just passively reading this all the way through and doing nothing with it. I didn't say *think* about what you want to accomplish in the next 90 days, I said *write it down*. I assure you that it is a much different level of experience when you get your eyes, hands, and brain working in concert to crystallize your goals. So for the last time: Do this with pen and paper, not just with your brain.

5. What you're writing will be *re-viewed*, so be honest with yourself and create some targets that will be fun for you to hit. Once you've got this base, we're going to design a whole program for self-accountability and programming,

so understand that you will be developing a relationship with these goals.

Enough description—time to get going. Get your pen and paper out and write down your five or six most important goals for the next 90 to100 days. Take as long as you need to do this, and then come back.

## Step 2—Identify the Keystone

Next, you're going to identify which of these is your "keystone goal." You may say, "What are you talking about? What the heck is a keystone goal?" Which is great, because it's likely that you've never looked at your goals this way.

Your keystone goal is the one goal that, by focusing *intensely* on its accomplishment, you support the majority of your other goals.

As you look at the handful of goals you wrote down, you likely notice that many of them are connected, and you may even realize that some are in competition with each other. But I've found that, in nearly every case, you'll see one of your goals from which, if you go after it hard, you'll likely get all the results you're looking for. I don't want to overcomplicate this. You may already know which one it is for you. It's actually quite common that when someone does what you've done thus far, one of the goals they write down just leaps off the page and rings in their brain, "Hey! Make me happen!" If you know now which one that is, just put a star by that one on your paper before you read the rest of this chapter.

If a keystone goal doesn't jump right out at you, that's all right too. I've had lots of times where I had to work out what my keystone would be, where the heaviest focus belonged. So again, what you're looking for is one of your goals that will most likely get you all of them. This can happen a few different ways. In some cases, your keystone goal will actually *create* the others as a byproduct, almost automatically. In other cases, your keystone goal will *require* the accomplishment of other goals as a stepping-stone or support mechanism. And in still other cases, your keystone goal may have such an impact on your life that you simply gain the power, confidence, and energy to knock down any wall you come up against. I'll give you an example.

Recently, I sat down to figure out what I really wanted to get out of the last 100 days of the year. I came up with the following:

1. Personal sales of $_____._____.
2. Personal income of $_____._____.
3. Pay off $_____ of debt.
4. Run 220 miles and strength train 35 times.
5. Meditate at least 50 times.
6. Take 14 days of guilt free, unplugged time off.

Those were the biggest ones. Notice that these are all very specific and easy to measure. I knew that I needed to boil this down into one goal that I became kind of obsessed with. There is technically no correct answer; none of these goals was better or worse than any of the others. It was just up to me to figure out where my most intent focus would pay the biggest dividends. Can you guess which one I chose? Well, I picked the sales goal. The number itself would not be helpful to know, but here's the thinking behind it. Hitting the sales goal would effectively create the income and the debt payoff automatically. Being on track for those would also allow for the vacation time nicely. What's the connection with the workouts and the meditating? I just knew that being on track with my physical, mental, and spiritual health is what would provide the energy and focus necessary. So they all work together. By consciously focusing on one keystone goal with all these connections, the subconscious actually goes to work on all of them, making them much more likely. You see?

So your next step is to do the same with your goals—determine which of yours is the key to all of them. If you don't have one of them starred already, take the time to decide which of your goals is going to be your keystone. And if you're a little baffled by this step, get in touch with me directly. Make sure you feel good about this one before moving on.

# Step 3—Solidify the Why

Now that you've got one objective to focus your mind on, it's time to answer the most important question of all: *Why?* More specifically, why is the accomplishment of this goal important to you? Here again, you may have the answer in a flash of intuition. Sometimes the stars line up and you just feel it. You're murmuring, "I don't need to over-think this. I have simply never been this stoked about my life and I am ready to go!" If that's going on, fantastic! Just take a moment and write down what you're thinking as an anchor.

If you don't have the bolt of lightning working for you, try these questions to stimulate your thinking:

- Why do I want to accomplish this?
- What will the accomplishment of this goal give me or do for me?
- How will I feel when I make this goal a reality? Confident? Excited? Peaceful? Pumped? Solid?
- How will pursuing this goal make me better or stronger? How will it require me to grow?
- When I get this result, what will I be able to do then?

When it comes to Why, there is no such thing as a wrong answer, and the more answers you have the better. Take some time with your pen and paper and answer the Why question for yourself.

## Step 4—Make It Visual

Your next step for heightening your focus and tuning up your mind is to make it visual. So far, everything we've done has involved your making plans. Most people never even get this far in thinking about goals, so you're already way ahead, but there's much more you can do to accelerate your progress. Your subconscious mind has literally billions of times the horsepower of your conscious mind. Additionally, it thinks and operates much differently than the conscious mind. As we discussed, one big key to unlocking the subconscious is to understand that it thinks in pictures. Where your conscious mind actually thinks coherent, linear, sequential thoughts (that actually sound like sentences in your mind), your subconscious essentially just sees pictures and moves powerfully toward them.

So to turn that on, give your brain something to see! Give it some pictures to work with. Sometimes I've had my clients put their visuals into a notebook or three ring binder. Sometimes I have them make a vision board where they can see all of their images at one time in their workspace. Lots of my clients will put visuals of their goals on index cards along with affirmations. There are tons of ways to make your goals visual—experiment to find what works for you.

## Step 5—Create Supporting Rituals

Step 5 in the process of heightening your focus is to create some rituals. When I say rituals I don't mean like chanting or sacrificing a goat. All I mean here is that you're going to consciously establish some automatic behavior patterns that anchor to and center on your goals. Please understand I am not just making this up. There are three books I've read over the years that have really hammered this step home for me. They are:

1. *The Power of Full Engagement*, by James E. Loehr and Tony Schwartz
2. *Get Out of Your Own Way*, by Robert K. Cooper
3. *The Answer*, by John Assaraf and Murray Smith

The first two really helped me understand the science of habits, and the third gave me a lot of the step-by-step program that is currently working well for me and my clients.

Are you aware that the vast majority of your thoughts are habitual? Dr. Deepak Chopra says that over 99 percent of the thoughts we have today are the exact same thoughts we had yesterday, and 99 percent of the thoughts we'll have tomorrow are the exact same thoughts we're having today. Since our thoughts essentially create our actions, this means that a lot of what we do—in our work, for our health, in our finances—we do habitually. It's automatic. Think about it: From the time you wake up in the morning until the time you get out the door to go to work, how often does your morning look essentially the same? Feet hit the ground, stumble out of bed, brush the teeth, shave, shower, coffee, get dressed, breakfast (maybe), more coffee, check the e-mail, more coffee, wake the kids, make their lunch, more coffee, out the door. Pay attention for a few mornings, and you might be surprised at how similar one day is to the next. So you already have these automatic behavior patterns; what I'll encourage you to do is to be conscious of them for a time and then establish a new habit pattern in their place, specifically at two times of the day.

The first is right away, immediately when you wake up in the morning. The first hour—specifically the first few moments—of your day is a very powerful time for programming your mind for success. The reason is that during that time your brain is transitioning from a sleeping state to a waking state, and your brain waves are configured in such a way that your subconscious mind is exceptionally receptive to the "thought seeds" that are planted.

Have you ever noticed how the first moments of your day seem to set the tone for the rest of it? Have you ever woken up on the wrong side of the bed? Pay attention, and you'll start to see the practical connections between a powerful start to the day and a powerful rest of the day. Most of us waste this window of opportunity on a bunch of stress or just semi-conscious fogginess. Many successful people purposefully use that first portion of the day as a way of tuning their mind for a heightened focus on their goals and dreams. It's true, you can make a decision to wake up on the *right* side of bed every day, and reap the rewards of starting the day right.

Chapter 17 of *Train Your Brain for Success* is entirely devoted to what we call the *Power Hour*, a daily energy management practice. If you'd like the complete rundown right now, feel free to jump to Chapter 17. The basics, however, are that I'll teach you a specific 15-step process that my clients and I use to create an undefeated mentality every day.

You may not want to adopt my specific 15 steps, which is fine. Maybe you don't like push-ups, or you prefer tea over coffee, or you have different videos that you like, or you only want to do 6 steps rather than 15. The vast majority of the world does zero steps. The point is to create your own conscious programming habits for the first hour of the day and stick to them diligently for 30 days. It will take that long to begin to rewire your brain, and by then you will be almost addicted to your Power Hour. It becomes fun!

The second time to be aware of your programming is the last few moments of your day. For many of the same reasons that the first hour is important, so are the last few minutes before drifting off. You brain experiences that transitional phase at the end of the day as well as at the beginning. What I encourage here is not nearly as complex as the Power Hour, but just as conscious. Sometime during the last hour of your day, just take a moment and re-view your goals and some affirmations, and then take a moment to express gratitude for anything positive that happened during the day. As a bonus, this is also a great time to think through your Daily Big Six (see Chapter 12) and lay out your most important objectives for the following day. You will key your thoughts for a restful night of sleep, very pleasant dreams, and a ton of energy the next morning.

A little programming goes a long way.

So there you have it—five specific steps that we know from experience will give you the kind of mental focus that top achievement requires. If you'll get started on them immediately and make them part of your daily and weekly routines, you cannot help but see improved results.

**Reinforcement and Bonuses:** This chapter has been Memory Optimized™ for your benefit. For your brief lesson and some great bonuses, visit www.planetfreedom .com/trainyourbrain with the access code on page 232. Enjoy!

# 9

## Overcoming Barriers

Anytime you try to get from point A to point B, stuff happens that can get you off track or slow you down, right? I have two young children, and it seems like anytime we try to go anywhere, stuff comes up immediately!

"Daddy, I forgot my giraffe!"
"Daddy, I have to pee!"
"Daddy, we forgot the permission slip!"

And on and on. It's nobody's fault, it's just life! I make light of this, but haven't you experienced this in your life? Not just trying to take a trip to the grocery store with kids—I mean anytime you try to take your life from where you are to where you really want to be. You've committed to lose 20 pounds and get in great shape, but somehow by the end of the first week you've already skipped going to the gym twice. Or you've decided to grow your business by 30 percent, but for some reason you just can't muster the motivation to make the calls. Or maybe you got off to a great start on some project, but illness or some other external circumstance derailed your progress. In my life and in the lives of our clients it seems that anytime we set out to do anything, obstacles pop up and slow us down or get us off track. Some of these obstacles come from outside of us, some come from inside of us, and some of them look like external circumstances but really we've created them unconsciously. The good news is that you can deal with them and get where you want to go, if you're prepared and have a game plan.

## Three Emotional Barriers

### Unwillingness to Accept 100% Responsibility

The first and most damaging is an unwillingness to accept 100 percent responsibility. Most people are simply not willing to accept that they are in charge of their life 100 percent. I am far from the first person to make this observation. In *The 7 Habits of Highly Effective People*, Stephen Covey talks extensively about accepting responsibility, or as he calls it: response-ability. In his outstanding book, *The Success Principles*, Jack Canfield makes accepting 100 percent responsibility for your life the very first chapter. The reason that so many of the greatest personal development thinkers of all time hammer on this principle so hard is that so many people miss it. The vast majority of human beings do not accept total responsibility for their actions or results. Yet taking this step is the first thing necessary for any growth to occur. I'm not saying that most of us accept zero responsibility—most people will admit that they have some role in the quality of their life—but for most of us the concept of *100 percent responsibility* is foreign.

How can you spot this barrier? Quite simply, it looks like *blaming*. If you've ever found yourself blaming a failure of any kind on the government, the economy, your stupid boss, your lazy employees, your spouse, the weather, your parents, your kids, your birth order, or any number of easy targets, you are dealing with this barrier. If you continue accepting anything less than 100 percent responsibility, you create what is known as a *victim mentality*. If you think and act like a victim, you simply won't get very far. You and you alone are responsible for the quality of your life.

It's helpful to distinguish between accepting *responsibility* and accepting *blame*. Accepting blame indicates that you did something wrong. Accepting responsibility is done for the specific purpose of dealing with reality. For example:

I have a family history of cancer. My father died at a relatively young age from colon cancer, and so did his mother. So there is a gene in the Seip family that lends itself to developing this disease, and almost certainly this gene was passed on to me. This is not my fault. It just is, and it makes no sense for anyone to blame me for this genetic predisposition. It makes even less sense for me to blame anyone else! What does make sense is to accept 100 percent *responsibility* for this circumstance, and do everything in my power to influence it. When I accept responsibility, I eat well, exercise regularly, learn how to care for my body, and get the appropriate tests done very early. Blame gets us nowhere. Accepting responsibility is the thing that enables us to move forward.

So how do we overcome this barrier? The very act of setting goals is one of the biggest things that we can do to cue our subconscious that we are in charge. Think about it—if we don't believe we're responsible for our outcomes, how could we possibly set goals at all? When you sit down, think about the future, set a goal, and begin working toward that goal, that very act is an act of taking responsibility. Whenever I've needed to get some aspect of my life back on track, just sitting down with myself and telling myself, "Okay, this is where we're going" is the first (and often only) step necessary to reassert who's in charge. The more frequently we do this, the better we train our minds to create our reality.

## Unwillingness to Look Foolish

The second emotional barrier to growth is an *unwillingness to look foolish*. This is also known as fear of criticism or fear of failure. Most of us are simply afraid to look bad in front of anyone else. This starts around late elementary school or middle school when fitting in becomes terribly important to us. It's detrimental because reaching our goals inherently involves two things—taking risks and getting out of our comfort zone. If we're held back by an unwillingness to look foolish, we can't do either.

How can you tell if you're dealing with this barrier? It manifests as *excuse-making*. If you've ever known (or been) someone who talks a good game but then always has an excuse when it comes time to actually perform, you recognize the classic sign of fear of looking foolish.

If you want the antidote to this barrier, it's simple: Develop a strategy and get over yourself! In the vast majority of cases, when we are afraid of looking foolish we are simply making up a fictional story. I was recently at a party with a friend who had just attended her 20-year reunion. These days she's pretty cool, but by her own admission she was not one of the cool kids in high school. So she bumped into a guy who had been very popular in high school. They didn't know each other well, but got to talking, and shortly my friend was shocked to hear this guy say, "Susan, I was always afraid to talk to you. I wanted to ask you out, but you just seemed way out of my league." Which was funny, because the whole time in school, she had been afraid to talk to him for the exact same reason!

My father used to say, "you wouldn't worry so much what other people think about you, if you realize how seldom they do." Really, who are all those people who you think will make fun of you? Most of them have their own problems and aren't paying attention at all. The rest would actually be totally supportive or even intimidated if they knew what you were shooting for.

For a first strategy, I would go all the way back to the five characteristics of an effective goal. Specifically, the first one: Make dead sure that you have selected goals that are meaningful to you. Second, do the things we discussed to heighten your focus. When you are chasing after something you are really passionate about you won't care what anyone thinks. When you devote your focus to achieving that goal and fill your mind with positive thoughts, you'll simply crowd out your fear. Third, a coach or accountability partner can be really helpful. Someone who you know is going to be supportive and cheer you on is an invaluable tool for overcoming your unwillingness to look foolish.

## Unwillingness to Take Action

Our third emotional barrier to achievement is an *unwillingness to take action*. To achieve the things you want requires *action*—in many cases, massive and immediate action. If you want to make sales, you will need to talk to some people. If you want to get in shape, you will need to get to the gym. If you want to get a date, you will need to ask. Nothing happens until you make something happen.

There are two common syndromes that identify this barrier. One is *procrastination*, the tendency to put things off. The other syndrome, just as common, is known as *analysis paralysis*. If you've ever known (or been) someone who gathers all the knowledge, does all the research, makes all the preparations, and then just never actually gets started, you're looking at an unwillingness to take action. These folks spend tons of time getting ready to get set, but never go. Analysis paralysis is really easy to disguise as good, rational, decision making. The trouble is that you end up being like someone who wants to go on a really great trip, but then waits for every light to turn green before they'll leave the driveway! You'll notice that successful people who hit their goals have a pretty strong tendency to "ready, fire, aim." I'm not saying make rash decisions; I'm saying most of us tend to err on the side of not enough action.

How do you overcome procrastination and analysis paralysis? Again, go back to the five characteristics of effective goals, this time characteristic number three. If your goals are the right size—big enough to challenge but small enough to be believable—that will help a lot. Much of this particular barrier comes from being intimidated or overwhelmed. If you've structured your goals in a way that you can clearly see the finish line, that helps you to feel confident.

Remember, just take the first step. And only after you've taken that step take the next. Everyone struggles to some degree with unwillingness to take action. I personally struggle with my own inertia in lots of areas. I have a lot of days when I need to make a few dozen sales calls and I don't want to. I have a lot of days when I plan to work out or run a few miles and I don't want to do it. And on and on, the point being that when I feel like this, I've learned that my feelings of distaste or intimidation disappear completely as soon as I actually start. Once I've made one or two calls, I suddenly want to make the rest of them. Once I've done the first quarter mile, the next four feel great. Action really does cure fear.

Here's a little incident I witnessed in a parking lot. A mother was walking out of a store with her son. The kid was somewhere around three years old, and was making it very clear that he did not want to get in the car.

"*I don't wanna! Noooo, I don't wanna!*"

His mom (who seemed to know this drill) said calmly, "You don't want to get in?"

"*No, I don't wanna!*"

She smiled and said, "That's fine. You don't have to wanna, you just have to do it. Let's go."

And the kid got in the car. We sometimes have to treat our own brains like that preschooler. You don't have to wanna, you just need to get going.

## Mental Barriers

### Inability to Stay on Track

One of the biggest mental blocks we struggle with is that we humans get sidetracked really easily. Sometimes any distraction will do.

"I know I need to get in shape, but that quart of ice cream in the freezer just looked so good. Oops."

"I know I need to pay off my credit cards, but I thought—well, just one more flat screen TV. Oops."

"Well, I know there's this part of my sales process that really gets good results, but I just forgot to do it six times in a row. Oops."

"I was going to write this book, but somehow I found myself playing spider solitaire for an hour. Oops!"

If it sounds like I am making fun of these, I am. Some of this is due to how our brains are wired, but a lot of this inability to stay on track is just a lack of clarity and specificity about what we want to accomplish.

So be extremely specific and clear in what your goals are. Nearly everyone needs to be much more specific in their thinking. For some reason, I usually have to take my clients and coax or berate them into thinking more specifically. I ask them to write out their goals and they come back with things like:

- Get in better shape.
- Sell more properties.
- Pay off debt.
- Go on vacation.

Which are fine, but they do nothing for your brain. Most people resist the idea of being specific in their objectives, so—don't be like most people. Remember Mort Utley?

"The reason most people don't get what they want is that they don't actually know what they want." Be smarter than that. Your brain needs something to focus on, and in the absence of a very clear and specific objective, it will always default to what is easiest and most immediate. So start with making your goals specific and clear.

A second strategy for staying on track goes back to something I said earlier about our wiring: Our brains are wired to notice and gravitate toward things that are different. If something is out of the ordinary, our natural programming forces us to pay attention to it. Back in the day, when something different was the shadow of a sabertooth tiger hunting us, this was really a helpful trait. Nowadays, it just leads us to be easily distracted. Your wiring is not your fault, but you are responsible for doing something about it. So here's the strategy:

Identify what commonly distracts you and *eliminate it*.

In the world of health and nutrition there's a saying: "Smart *eating* begins with smart *shopping*." If you have junk to eat in your house, you will eventually end up eating it, just because it's there and it's easy. In the world of building wealth, one of the most basic principles is to pay yourself first—take a percentage of your income every month and set it aside where you can't get it easily. Both of these strategies work so well it's almost like magic. But it's not magic, it just makes sense. If you eliminate the ability to make poor choices, you make many fewer poor choices.

Here's the key: When you do this, *you don't even notice the difference. You only notice the drastically improved result.* When I don't have junk food in my house, I hardly even notice it isn't there. I just have a snack that doesn't wreck my body. And if I ever do think, "Hmmmm, I'd really love some Cheetos," it's too much trouble to actually go get them. So it ends up being just a passing thought, rather than a couple of thousand calories' worth of saturated fat going into my body. I don't notice the pain; I just notice when the doctor says, "Wow, your blood pressure is the lowest I've ever seen." When I first started saving 10 percent of my income, I noticed zero difference in my day-to-day quality of life. I had just as much fun, did just as much cool stuff, and enjoyed my life at least as much as before. I just noticed that at year end I had several thousand dollars growing in some investments. Amazing.

So make the commitment right now to eliminate what gets you off track. If you need to clean out your fridge, do it. If TV is sucking your energy and you need to cancel cable, do it. If you need to stop responding within five seconds to every e-mail, shut off the alarm that says, "You've got mail." Whatever is getting you off track will *continue* getting you off track until you *eliminate it*, so eliminate it. It will be less painful than you think. Day to day you won't notice the difference—you'll just notice when you start hitting your goals with much greater frequency and speed.

## Overwhelm/Overthinking/Too Much Pressure

The last mental barrier that I wanted to address is the issue of being overwhelmed by your goals, or putting too much pressure on yourself. Most people tend to freak themselves out, which hurts performance. In our memory training workshops, we talk about how "stress is the number one killer of your memory." Well, the same thing goes for any area where performance is important. A small amount of pressure can be helpful in providing energy, but negative stress or too much pressure can really shut down your brain. And a lot of the stress we experience is self-generated. We actually create our stress through what I call overthinking. There's a kind of relaxed intensity that gets results. There's a great story about Franz Klammer, the Olympic downhill skier. Going into his final run, Klammer was in contention, but behind enough that he needed to essentially break the course record to win the gold. Before his run he was laughing and joking around. When the gates opened, he made one of the ugliest runs of the whole Olympic games. His start was technically wrong and he looked like he was about to wipe out for much of the run. At the bottom, however, he had done what he needed. He broke the course record and won the gold!

Afterwards, all the reporters wanted to analyze his performance. They wanted know what he was thinking, why he did what he did, and so on. And he just didn't have an answer. They kept asking stuff like, "Why didn't you push harder on your poles out of the gate?" and "Why did you take that angle on such and such curve?" Klammer just kept having to say "You know, I don't know, I didn't really think about it." Finally, when pressed for an answer to the question "Come on, you had to be thinking about something—what was it?" His answer was:

"Going fast, I guess."

There's a time for thinking and a time for letting go of thinking, so here are a couple of strategies for facilitating this relaxed intensity.

*First of all, do your thinking all at once.* When you are in the middle of doing what you need to do, that's not the time for conscious thinking. Some people have what I'll call "leftover thinking," when the time has come to be performing (time to let the subconscious take over), but they're still thinking (consciously). Usually this happens because of a nagging suspicion that "I'm not ready yet, I'm not prepared." Do all your thinking at once, then pull the trigger.

Secondly, to eliminate being overwhelmed, take your goals and *break them down into bite-size pieces.* For example, I recently set a quarterly sales goal that was going to be about 35 percent bigger than my biggest sales quarter ever. At first, thinking about it kind of made me gulp; it was a bit intimidating to think of it all in one piece. But when I broke it down to specifically how many presentations I would need to give, how many phone calls I would have to make, and how much business I would need to generate per client, I realized, "Well I can totally do that!" When I then broke that down to what I would need to do each week and each day, my confidence skyrocketed because I saw that the daily activities were actually well within my comfort zone. You'll find that if you take your end goal and think backwards from it—sort of "reverse engineer" it down to specific activities—it's amazing how you get rid of that overwhelming and overthinking that can be so crippling. Once you have a plan that's specific, then you can shut off the thinking and just execute. Fun!

Here's a last strategy for overwhelming/overthinking and too much pressure—*make it a game!* Really, one of the biggest things that trips people up is that they put too much pressure on themselves. So make it a little less serious—everyone loves a good game. So make a game of your goals! Here are two of my favorites.

One is the thermometer game. I'll take my goals, break them down as I just described, and then I'll take the goals and subgoals and make them into a thermometer, with 0 at the bottom and whatever the number is at the top. The game then just becomes to see how fast I can fill up the thermometer. Does that sound silly? Maybe, but it sure is effective. Your very powerful, very visual, very simpleminded subconscious understands "fill up the thermometer" in a way that works, and is fun. Try it out.

My other favorite is the small rewards game. Here you set up benchmarks along the way to your ultimate goal, and when you get there, you get a small reward. For example, in my sales goal that I talked about before, at 20 percent of it I agreed (with myself) to get a new pair of glasses. At 30 percent I agreed to take my wife out for a really nice dinner. At 50 percent my reward was a new suit. Nothing succeeds like success, and we just perform better when we can clearly see what we're working for. Your rewards can be whatever you like—a charitable donation, a piece of jewelry, a long weekend, a spa treatment—just make it something that you would really like. Try this out next time you've got a goal that seems a little out of your comfort zone. Reward and congratulate yourself at specific points along the way, and just see how much more momentum you build.

**Reinforcement and Bonuses:** This chapter has been Memory Optimized™ for your benefit. For your brief lesson and some great bonuses, visit www.planetfreedom .com/trainyourbrain with the access code on page 232. Enjoy!

# Component #2

# Being Fully Present: Using Time as It's Meant to Be Used

# 10

# Common Myths of Time Management and How to Use Time as It's Meant to Be Used

How many of the following days have you experienced?

- The day where you were extremely busy all day, but then at the end of the day wondered what you really accomplished.
- The day where you were extremely bored all day, and at the end of the day wondered what you really accomplished.
- The day where you were at work all day but could only think about what was happening at home; then as soon as you went home you could only think about work.
- The day you really planned to work on an important project all day, then spent the entire day dealing with one interruption after another, and the day just slipped away.

- The day that was spent in boring meeting after boring meeting, and just slipped away
- The day where you just spun your wheels and got frustrated.

If any of these sound familiar, pay attention, because *these days will keep happening to you until you do something different*. It's likely that you are suffering from some common misconceptions about how time functions and how we function in time. Some of these misconceptions stem from how we're wired, some stem from how society conditions us, and some of them just are. Either way, here are the most common myths of time management, and how to reframe your understanding.

## The Myth of Balance

Think about the important areas of your life, the overall categories that demand your attention, time, and energy. You have the following categories, in no particular order.

- Physical—caring for your body, health, and physical space.
- Mental/emotional/spiritual—caring for your mind/spirit.
- Financial—caring for your money.
- Professional—taking care of business.
- Family—taking care of those who are closest to you.
- Community/social—taking care of the people you care about who aren't family.

It's a lot of places to direct your energy, and many people come to our workshops because they want to achieve "balance." I tell them:

*The desire to achieve "balance" is your first problem.*

Balance doesn't exist in our society, and even if it did you wouldn't want it. We're talking about time here, so let's consider what perfect balance would look like. There are 24 hours in a day, so a perfectly balanced life would mean that each of the six areas listed above would get exactly four hours per day, no more and no less. "Well, that's ridiculous, you have to take a longer time horizon than one day," you say. Okay, let's look at a balanced week. Every week has 168 hours, so a balanced week would have:

28 hours of exercise and/or sleep.

28 hours of reading, prayer, meditation, and/or learning of some kind.

28 hours of investing/financial planning.

28 hours of work.

28 hours of quality time with family.

28 hours of quality time with friends and/or community.

See what I mean? A life of balance would actually suck. So stop fretting over your own lack of balance—embrace it! You don't actually want balance in your life, what you want is *harmony*. Harmony means that you accept that your life will be unbalanced—it's your job to simply make it unbalanced in the way that works for you. It's a much more natural way to live.

## The Myth that Time Can Be Managed

People use the term time management all the time. Famous gurus and entire companies have been built to teach people how to manage time more effectively. Many of those gurus or companies teach great stuff; much of it has impacted me tremendously. But if we are to break records in our lives we need to be clear. Napoleon Hill cited "accurate thinking" as one of his 15 Laws of Success. So to be perfectly accurate, time cannot be managed. It just keeps rolling right along. You can't fire time, you can't give time a performance review and alter its behavior, can't change time's bonus structure to get more effort out of it. You can't manage time, so stop trying!

Instead, focus on what you can manage. Keep in mind the C.I.A model of thinking. C.I.A means that in life there are things you must:

**Control**

**Influence**

**Accept**

When we learn to accept the things we have no control or influence over, we take away resentment. When we control the controllables and influence the influenceables, our lives take a quantum leap forward. The flow of time is one thing that we all have to accept. How we act, how we prioritize, and how we focus are what we either control or influence. Manage those and you are dealing with time as you are meant to.

## The Myth of "Enough" Time

How many times have you ever said to anyone, "I just didn't have enough time," or "There's not enough time"? Once again, this is a common phrase that is patently false. It's important to understand that thinking in terms of "not enough time"—the thinking itself—is a trap. When you think in terms of "not enough" anything it creates what's called a *scarcity mentality*. A scarcity mentality, all by itself, can drain your energy to a point that is difficult to overcome.

Here are two ways of debunking this myth.

1. Mathematically: As we discussed, there are exactly 168 hours in your week. No more, no less. Consider the richest person on planet earth—how many hours does he get per week? Exactly 168. Now consider the poorest person in the poorest country on earth—how many hours in his week? You got it—168. Nobody gets any more (or any less) time

than anyone else. So the whole concept of "enough" time doesn't even compute.

2. Experientially: Come on now, you don't actually need me to keep throwing the 168 hours number around, do you? You know from your own life the whole concept of "not enough" time is just a story. I was with a client recently who is a full-time minister, runs a catering business, and has six children. When we discussed this concept of "not enough" time he had a visible a-ha moment. I asked him what had just happened in his brain, and he said, "I just realized that I either have or make time for everything that's important to me—everything." And the same is true for all of us. We either have or make time for every single thing that's important to us. The real deal with "not enough" time is that we allow things that are not really important to us—TV, video games, booze, drama, oversleeping, other people's problems—to become important to us in a given moment.

## What Exactly Is Time Management Then?

So if the concept of balance, of not enough time, and in fact the whole concept of time management itself are just myths, what the heck are we talking about here? How you deal with your time is in fact one of the most critical components of a record-breaking life, so let's revisit something that was mentioned in our discussion of the CIA model. If you want to get great at using your time effectively, you'll really be managing:

1. Your priorities—You and you alone must decide what's most important to you.

2. Your focus—You and you alone must determine where you put your attention at any given moment.

3. Your activities—Ultimately, you and you alone must decide what you do with any given moment, hour, day, or week.

In Chapter 11, you'll be taught a specific, step-by-step process for bringing your priorities, your focus, and your activities into line. For now, let's understand a little more deeply.

## Understanding Importance versus Urgency

We often get trapped into focuses and activities that make us feel good for the moment but don't actually get us very far. A big part of why is that we get caught in the tyranny of the urgent.

Any activity that we engage in has two components: its importance and its urgency. It's critical to understand that these are not the same. Importance answers the question, "How much impact does this have on my life?" Urgency only answers the question, "How soon must this happen?" These are totally different and separate questions.

President Dwight Eisenhower is credited with first naming this way of understanding our actions. In *The 7 Habits of Highly Effective People*, Stephen Covey made this model well known, but it's known as the "Eisenhower Matrix," and it's essential to understand it. It looks like Figure 10.1.

I'm hardly the first person to point out the obvious conclusion, which is that you want to spend as much time in Quadrant 2 as possible, but I'll take it a step further. *Quadrants 1, 3, and 4 will actually kill you*, just in different ways and at different speeds.

### Quadrant 1

Here you find activities that are both important (high impact) and urgent (need to be addressed now). These are life's emergencies. If you've ever spent a day in Quadrant 1 you ended up tired, but it was a good tired. You successfully put out fires and came through in the clutch. You had a pressure filled scenario to deal with and you came through! You feel like a rock star when you succeed in Quadrant 1, and herein lies the big trap. Living in Quadrant 1 can be highly addictive, and if you spend too much time there you

| Quadrant 1 | Quadrant 2 |
|---|---|
| IMPORTANT and URGENT | IMPORTANT but not urgent |
| Examples: Heart attack, impending deadline, taxes on April 14th | Examples: Exercise, goal setting, taxes on January 15th |
| Time spent here will feel great but burn you out–be careful. | Time INVESTED here reduces time spent in all the other quadrants–it also feels awesome! |
| Kills you by hemorrhaging your energy. | |
| Quadrant 3 | Quadrant 4 |
| URGENT but not important | Not urgent and not important |
| Examples: Interruptions, other people's problems | Examples: Unconscious TV watching, gossip, other time wasters |
| Time spent here leaves you feeling busy/tired, but really frustrated and unproductive. | Time spent here is just boring. |
| Kills you by drowning you in minutia. | Kills you by strangling your soul. |

**Figure 10.1** The Eisenhower Matrix

will eventually fail. Either you'll get into an emergency that you can't handle, or you'll just burn out. Quadrant 1 is exhilarating, but it's very stressful. It's really helpful to be able to succeed here, but it's not a healthy way to live.

### Quadrant 3

You know that there are things that simply suck up your time and energy with little to no reward. This is Quadrant 3, what Covey called the "Quadrant of deceit." In Quadrant 3 you get fooled into thinking that what you're doing is important, but at the end of the day you realize that you didn't get anywhere. A day spent here leaves you feeling tired and empty.

In today's age of instant access, it's very easy to waste an entire week, month, or your whole life in Quadrant 3. If you do not learn to establish boundaries and then enforce them, if you don't learn to say "no" to certain activities and people, here's what happens:

*Interruptions and other people's problems will consume your life. Your entire life. And it will happen because you let it happen.*

Fortunately, it doesn't have to happen. Getting clear on your goals, implementing the Two-Hour Solution and then taking care of your mind, as you'll learn about in Chapters 11 and beyond, will keep you out of this trap, but you must be vigilant. If I'm overselling this so be it; I've just seen too many people waste years in Quadrant 3. Stay out of it.

### Quadrant 4

Quadrant 4 consists of activities that are neither important nor urgent. They have little or no impact on your life, and nobody cares if you ever do them. Things like mindless channel surfing, mindless game playing, checking your credit score for the third time this week, or any number of simple time wasters live here. I don't feel the need to describe this one in detail because you know when you fall into this trap. All I will say about Quadrant 4 is that this one will kill your career, your health, your relationships, your finances, and your ambition—and you won't even enjoy it. When you find yourself in Quadrant 4, *do anything else.* Just get moving in some direction other than the one where you're currently heading.

Life in Quadrants 1, 3, and 4 will kill you one way or the other, so let's look at the only quadrant that's ultimately an investment of time rather than an expense.

### Quadrant 2

These are activities that are *important* but not *urgent.* The things that really make the big difference in your life usually start with deadlines that are far away, or (more commonly) there just is no deadline. Things like physical exercise, spending quality time with family, setting goals, reading, praying, and so on are the activities that really impact and enrich our lives, and *you'll never finish them*. You'll do them forever, and you'll want to because they feed you rather than drain you. A day invested in Quadrant 2 leaves you feeling like you really did something great for your life. You'll have more energy at the end of the day than you did at the beginning.

It's been said that what is truly important is usually not urgent, and vice versa. The trap we fall into is that our brains are not wired to respond to what is important—our brains are wired to react to what is urgent. To make matters worse, we live in a culture that reinforces this reactive approach. Add it up and it means that if you are to invest your time in things that are actually important, *you will need a system*.

That's where we're going next.

Chapter 11 will teach you the Two-Hour Solution, which is a comprehensive approach to creating your schedule. Implementing the Two-Hour Solution will definitely take time out of where it's killing you and put it where it will lift you up. Before we leave this chapter, however, let's get the foundation of your time usage system in place.

Your system begins with the right questions.

## The Most Important Time Management Questions

Want a two-minute action step that will boost your time usage for the rest of your life?

Write the following three questions on a notecard and place them in a prominent spot.

1. What quadrant am I in right now?
2. Is what I'm doing right now moving me toward my goals?
3. Is this the best use of my time right now?

That's it—just three questions on a notecard—does that seem too simple? Don't be deceived, these three questions are incredibly powerful for training your brain, and regardless of the answers, the questions themselves create no-lose situations for you. All of them do the same powerful things for your brain that the three Smart Reading questions did. More on the power of good questions in Chapter 14, but these three are fantastic. Mainly, they heighten your awareness—you cannot escape a trap you don't know you're in. Just by heightening your awareness, you *automatically* direct your RAS to start working for you. When you identify what quadrant you're in, you *automatically* activate your brain to look for a more productive path. When you ask if your current activities are moving you toward your goals, you *automatically* become more aware of your goals. When you ask if your current activities really are the best use of your time, you *automatically* become more aware of what the best path would be. The best news is that when you ask, even if your answers are unsatisfactory to you, the questions themselves make your time usage more effective. Ask yourself just these three questions a few times a day for a week and you'll notice that you make healthy adjustments to your activities much more quickly. Do that consistently for three weeks and you'll develop positive momentum in every area of your life.

So once again—if you haven't done so already, get those three questions on a notecard right now. Better yet, make one for your office, one for your home, and one for your car. Put them up one time, and heighten your time awareness forever.

In summary, it's really easy to get caught up in myths and incorrect premises about the time we have. Everyone gets the exact same 168 hours each week. You can't manage time, but you can manage yourself—your activities and your focus. When you take charge of that, your life improves dramatically. Chapters 11 and 12 will show you specifically how to do that.

**Reinforcement and Bonuses:** This chapter has been Memory Optimized™ for your benefit. For your brief lesson and some great bonuses, visit www.planetfreedom .com/trainyourbrain with the access code on page 232. Enjoy!

# 11

## The Two-Hour Solution: How To Create a Record-Breaking Schedule

H ave you ever found 20 bucks in your dryer? I love it when that happens. Even though I am fully aware that the money was already mine, I didn't know it was there until I found it. So it feels like I got an unexpected blessing from the universe!

With that in mind . . .

Would you be willing to invest two hours each week, if that investment were guaranteed to give you back 10 hours in that same week? Loaded question, I know; if you answered no you wouldn't be reading this. But I'm serious; that's what this chapter will do for you if you'll implement what you learn. If I were only allowed to teach one practice that would dramatically boost a human being's performance and enjoyment of life, it would be what's in this chapter. It's called the Two-Hour Solution, and it's *the lynchpin* for someone who wants to break records. For me it's the wellspring from which a life lived on purpose flows.

I've been doing this rigorously since the age of 25, and it's one of only three perfect correlations I've noticed between activity and results. The other two will be discussed in Chapters 15–17 on Aggressive Mental Care, but the Two-Hour Solution is the first. What I mean by "perfect correlation" is that when I do this, my life goes well. Not necessarily perfectly, but well. To reinforce the correlation, I've found that if my life isn't going the way I want—if my business results are down, if I'm not as high-energy as I like, if I'm stressed out, if my relationships are suffering—I can always trace it back to being lax or ineffective with my Two-Hour Solution time.

In addition, when our coaching clients begin implementing the Two-Hour Solution, they discover a minimum of 10 more productive hours in every single week. Usually it's more like 20 or 30 hours, but in 15 years of teaching this I've never heard less than 10. I mean that the Two-Hour Solution will cause you to take at least 10 hours per week from Quadrants 1, 3, and 4 and put them where you really want them to be. We said in the last chapter that you can't manage time, but the Two-Hour Solution will make you feel like you are actually creating time that wasn't there before. It'll feel like finding 20 bucks in the dryer, only better!

I'm still underselling the value of this practice. The Two-Hour Solution is not just some trick that makes you feel good; it produces some of the most tangible and powerful bottom line results we see with our clients. I think about one executive we coached who told us in his coaching summary that this one system paid for his several thousand dollar coaching investment approximately 40 times over, in the first year. I think about one production manager I coached, and watched the Two-Hour Solution drop 20 pounds off his frame, deepen his spiritual life, and earn him a promotion much faster than he expected. I think about the hundreds of sales professionals we've taught this to, that when they make the investment of two hours per week, their earnings rise by 30 percent, 50 percent, in some cases 300 percent. I could go on and on, the point being that what you are about to learn is not theory. When you do it, it works. And even when it doesn't work, it still works! Even if you don't get exactly the results you were looking for, at a bare minimum the Two-Hour Solution puts you in the driver's seat of your life. Even if your week doesn't happen exactly as you planned (it rarely will), you end up much better off than if you hadn't made the investment. You really can't lose on this one, so let's get into it.

## The Two-Hour Solution Defined

Stephen Covey famously said that "all things are created twice—first in our minds and then in our external reality." The example used most frequently is that of a building. The architect created the building first in his mind, then drew up the blueprints, and only then did construction begin. But this concept is true for anything and everything manmade. A farm field, a car, this book you're reading, anything that was created by a human being was created first in somebody's mind, and then brought forth into the world.

Your life is the same way. You create your life first in your mind, and then you bring it forth. The key to understand is that this "mental creation" is happening whether you realize it or not. For most people, the problems in their life stem from the fact that the mental creation happens *accidentally*. They are not influencing the creation, it's just happening at a level below their awareness.

Know what else is the same way? Your week. You create your week first in your mind, then you execute it. Again, the mental creation of your week is *happening* whether you influence it or not. When you fail to exercise that influence, what happens is that your week runs you, rather than you running your week. Can you relate?

The Two-Hour Solution is a specific, seven-step method of investing *two hours per week*, for the purpose of *mentally creating* the next two weeks of your life. Statistically, very few people devote this level of time or thinking to creating their week. Only the most successful people do this.

Remember the principle of success leaves clues? Look at the most successful people in your field, and you will see that they do this. They may not call it the Two-Hour Solution, but they plan, they think, and they visualize. They mentally create their days, their weeks, their lives. They do it consciously, and they do it consistently. You do it too, and you will see similar results.

Here's how.

## How Do I Start?

The mechanics of the Two-Hour Solution are deceptively simple. You begin with simply setting aside a two-hour block of uninterrupted time for yourself. Ideally it's a single block. Two one-hour blocks can also work, but ideally you give yourself a single two-hour block of time. Keep in mind that the purpose of this time is to mentally create a stretch of your life. This is not just "make a to-do list," it's not just some drudging chore—it's creative time. Creative time usually requires a bit of a warm-up period for the juices to really get flowing. Don't make the mistake of thinking "Oh, I'll just squeeze it in here or there—I'm sure half an hour will be enough." The whole point here is that you are investing time in yourself, and it's the surest, most certain investment you can make. Believe me, you'll want at least two hours to do this right.

This should happen sometime *between the end of one workweek and the beginning of the next.* I've coached lots of executives who love to make their two hours the last two hours of the week on Friday afternoon. For me, Friday afternoon doesn't work well, but I love to be up early. So Saturday morning before my family wakes up is perfect for me. Lots of my clients choose to do this on Sunday evening as they transition from enjoying the weekend to prepping for a great week. You choose when works best for you, but get yourself some quiet uninterrupted time when you can shut off noise and just think.

## Why Do I Resist This?

Before we go any further, let me tell you what you may be thinking right now.

"Two hours?! Are you nuts? I can't afford to take two hours to just sit around and contemplate my navel, I have stuff to do!"

And I get it. We live in a society where other people create constant demands on our time, so it's really easy to experience feelings of guilt. Combine that with your mind's natural tendency to resist anything that's different, and I understand that it may feel somewhat uncomfortable to set aside this block of time, especially at first.

If this thought occurred to you, pay close attention to what I'll say next.

If you genuinely believe you can't afford a two-hour block of time for yourself, then you can't afford not to take that block, because you are a disaster waiting to happen. Ever flown in a commercial airliner? Think about what the flight attendant says about what to do if the oxygen masks come down. Whose mask must you put on first? That's right, yours. The reason for this is that if you try to help everyone else before you take care of yourself, you render yourself useless. You actually make the situation worse. The same goes for your life. If you really want to live a record-breaking life, if you really want to be able to best serve the people you care about, you must be able to think and create. This will not happen without you making it happen.

Consider what Gandhi said: "I pray for two hours every morning. If I have an exceptionally busy day ahead of me, then I pray for three hours." Speaking from experience, you will be very glad you made this investment. So will everyone else your life.

## What Do I Do with My Two Hours?

Once you've got the time set aside, sit down with the planning tool of your choice. You can use Outlook, Google Calendar, iCal, or whatever digital tool you prefer. Or you can go old-school with Day Timer, Day Runner, Priority Manager; any paper based system works too. For a look at a free Two-Hour Solution two-week worksheet, check out the bonuses at the end of this chapter. Feel free to use any tool you choose; just be sure that you can look at an entire week all at once. You're going to mentally create your upcoming week in quite a bit of detail, and at least paint the broad strokes on the following week, so be sure you can see a whole week at a time.

### Step 1. Reconnect with Your Goals

If you're not clear on what you want to accomplish, how you run your week is irrelevant. So before you do anything, take 5 or 10 minutes and review your goals. Take your keystone goal and visualize its accomplishment. See it vividly, and enjoy the excitement of seeing your goals come true. Contemplate all the good things that will come from it. Be grateful for the ability to mentally create your life—it's one of the things that makes you fundamentally human.

### Step 2. Review and Block Off Your Commitments

Once you've reviewed your goals and tuned up your brain, it's time to actually look at your next two weeks. Your commitments are the meetings or appointments that you already have planned to attend. Any time where you've agreed to be somewhere for or with somebody lives here. Your commitments probably will already be blocked off on your calendar—if not, put them in so you can see them. At the same time, think about how you'd like each meeting or appointment to turn out.

Some good questions to ask yourself are:

- What are your desired outcomes?
- Should this meeting be happening at all?
- Are the right people scheduled to be at this?
- How can this time be made most effective?
- Should this block of time be shortened (likely), or perhaps lengthened?
- What kind of prep do I need to do for this?

I devote this intense level of questioning to the upcoming week. The following week will get a less detailed look, because I know I'll be revisiting it during my next Two-Hour Solution time.

If you'll even just give this step your 100 percent attention and ask a few good questions of yourself, you'll be doing what the most successful do. You'll also put yourself ahead of at least 90 percent of your competition by doing this. Most people don't do any of it, which is why they don't get where they want to go.

### Step 3. Schedule Excellence Time

The very next thing to put in is your *excellence time*. If you recall from the previous chapter, excellence is the word we use to describe Quadrant 2. So excellence time is the time that you invest to strengthen yourself and your relationships. This is the time that builds you. Lots of things can live here; for me it's exercise, reading, meditating, and my planning/goal setting time. That's right, your next Two-Hour Solution session needs to get scheduled! You could also include mindful time with family or friends, community service, church, or any number of activities.

The big key here is that *these types of activities must be scheduled, and they must be scheduled before most other activities*. Why? Two reasons. Number one: If you don't give them the highest level of urgency they simply don't happen. For me, even when

I *do* give them the highest priority they sometimes don't happen. If you allow these types of activities to be an afterthought (as most people do), it's likely they will *never* happen. Life will get in the way. Number two: When you've planned to do it, you remove the guilt. You'll see as your Two-Hour Solution unfolds that you have plenty of time for everything that's important. In fact, you'll probably be surprised to learn that you have an enormous abundance of time for all of the amazing things you want to do, if you will just plan them. When that clicks, you no longer are held back by the guilty feelings that come with a scarcity mentality.

Put excellence time in your schedule—it makes your life awesome.

### Step 4. Schedule Your Green Time

Next up is "green time." This is specific to your professional life. It's called that because green is the color of *money*. In your work, there are only a small number of activities that directly make you money or that you get paid for. If you're an executive, it's running your company or department, *and that's it*. If you're a salesperson, it's selling, *and that's it*. If you're an athlete, it's practicing and playing, *and that's it*. Even in a large bureaucratic organization, *there is one reason you are on the payroll, and that's it*.

One reason most people feel pulled in too many directions at work is that they aren't clear on what that one reason—their green time—is. If you aren't clear, ask someone who knows. If you are clear (and if you're honest with yourself you probably are), commit to when you're going to make that time happen and then guard that time. If you will gain clarity on what your green time consists of, when the best time to engage in it is, and then dive into it with laserbeam focus, you and your colleagues will be shocked to see how much you can accomplish in a very short period.

### Step 5. Schedule Your Red Time

Red time is also part of your professional life—it's the time that doesn't directly get you paid, but does support your green time. There are things that need to happen before your green time to make it effective. There are also things that need to be done after your green time to either account for or deliver what your green time produced. Things like research, prep work for a presentation, organizing leads, paperwork, performance reviews, and other support activities live under red time. Lots of our clients identify it as "administrative time." We call it red time because red is the signal to stop. If red time is not done well, it stops your green time from being effective.

The key here is that while red time is important, it is not green time. The two are not the same and should be kept separate. This is not as easy as it sounds, because red time is usually much easier emotionally than green time. I've seen salespeople waste entire weeks "doing research" or "networking" when what they really needed to do was just pick up the phone and make a call. I've seen executives waste days "preparing a presentation" when they really just needed to have a 15-minute conversation with a problem-child manager. And on and on. Red time is important, but avoid the easy trap of letting it consume your more important green time. Green time is all about being effective because it usually involves dealing with people. Red time is all about being efficient.

So to make it as efficient as possible, put it in your schedule and do it in batches. Answer all of your e-mail at one time, do your paperwork at a preordained time, and so on. Doing it all at once rather than "a little here, a little there" drastically reduces the amount of time red time sucks up.

### Step 6. Schedule (or at Least Notice) Your Flex Time

Through steps one to five, look at everything you've got planned. By this point you will have reviewed your goals, visualized success, thought through, and blocked out the time for all of the stuff you need to do in the upcoming week, and most if not all of the stuff you really want to do. Congratulations! Here's a beautiful thing about the Two-Hour Solution: When you get here, you will notice significant chunks of your week where nothing is planned. It looks like the chart in Figure 11.1.

| Time | Sun | Mon | Tue | Wed | Thu | Fri | Sat |
|------|-----|-----|-----|-----|-----|-----|-----|
| 4 A.M. | | | | | | | |
| 5 A.M. | | Power Hour | | Power Hour | | | |
| 6 A.M. | | work out | Power Hour | work out | Power Hour | Power Hour | |
| 7 A.M. | | kids to school | kids to school | kids to school | kids to school | kids to school | |
| 8 A.M. | | drive to office | drive to Milwaukee | write report | | | |
| 9 A.M. | | staff meeting | | research | radio interview | follow-up calls | kids to basketball |
| 10 A.M. | | staff meeting | presentation | sales calls | | follow-up calls | kids to basketball |
| 11 A.M. | | | presentation | sales calls | | shoot promo videos | kids to basketball |
| 12 A.M. | | | presentation | | | | |
| 1 P.M. | | coaching session | | | | | |
| 2 P.M. | | coaching session | | sales calls | conf call w/Eric | review weekly stats | |
| 3 P.M. | | | drive back | sales calls | conf call w/Eric | 2 hours solution | |
| 4 P.M. | | coaching session | work out | | work out | 2 hours solution | run |
| 5 P.M. | | | kids to karate | | kids to karate | | |
| 6 P.M. | | | kids to karate | | kids to karate | family fun night | |
| 7 P.M. | | | | date night | | family fun night | |
| 8 P.M. | review week with Shan | | | date night | | family fun night | |
| 9 P.M. | | | | date night | | | |
| 10 P.M. | | | | | | | |
| 11 P.M. | | | | | | | |
| | | | | | | | |
| | | | | | | | |

**Figure 11.1** A Typical Week for Me

See the holes? Even the busiest people have them—an hour here, three hours there, another block someplace else. It's amazing how when someone thinks through a week, they end up with all the important stuff accounted for and then a bunch of extra time! All by itself, this simple awareness can really boost your abundance mentality. If you are wise, you set these unused *blocks aside as flex time.* Flex time gives you a "bucket" of time, into which you can put whatever you want. Ongoing projects, meetings/appointments that get scheduled last minute, some extra excellence or green time. Anything can be put into flex time—that's what it's there for!

The real beauty of having flex time is that it gives you what you need to stay the course. One of the big things that gets people off track is that they diligently plan out a week, get really excited about all the greatness they'll achieve, and then early Monday morning—*Boom*—some unforeseen crisis happens and blows up the morning. If there's no flexibility built in, it's too easy to say, "Well, there goes my plan—this scheduling thing clearly doesn't work." You end by giving up on the whole process and "throwing the baby out with the bathwater." With flex time built in, it becomes much easier to do what's healthy and realize that you've already considered that something like this could occur and then execute your backup plan. Simply take what you were intending to do when you got thrown off and put it into some of your already scheduled flex time. When you put it in flex time, you prevent the unplanned from wrecking your plan, and you dramatically boost your peace of mind.

### Step 7. Schedule Your Re-Creation Time

Last but not least, make absolutely sure that you have some recreation (or, more accurately, *re-creation*) time planned for yourself. It's likely that you already have some in (your excellence time often is recreational in nature), but if you haven't scheduled time to take care of yourself—mind, body, and spirit—do not miss the opportunity to put some in your calendar every week. If you don't take care of you, who will?

There you have it: the Two-Hour Solution. A specific, seven-step method of investing *two hours per week*, for the purpose of *mentally creating* the next two weeks of your life. Do it weekly, do it regularly, and watch your life improve.

## What about the Rest of the Week?

The Two-Hour Solution lays the foundation for the week, tunes up your subconscious mind to attract success, and then does one other thing—it provides context. People often ask us, "Should I also have a daily to-do list?" Absolutely. I recommend taking 10 to 15 minutes each day to think through your day and make necessary adjustments to the plan you created. More on this in Chapter 12, but the practice of thinking through your day *in the context* of a Two-Hour Solution planned week now makes your to-do list a very powerful tool instead of just a boring chore. Yes, you will need to make adjustments (remember that a plane is off course 90 percent of its flight), so feel free to make these changes.

At the end of your week then, take a few minutes to review. How did your plan work out? Did you get the results you wanted? Specifically, two questions are helpful here:

1. Was my plan effective?
2. How effective was I at sticking to my plan?

The good news is that when you answer these questions, you are guaranteed a positive outcome and you train positive momentum into your brain. If you got the results you were looking for, these questions will help you reproduce and improve upon those results. Even if your results were not what you hoped, you have the ability to determine where the problem occurred and decide how it's going to be different next week. Life is about learning, and structuring your weeks around the Two-Hour

Solution will make you much more mindful of the lessons that you need to learn now.

Ready to take this structure and supercharge its effectiveness? Chapter 12 will give you some great strategies for making your time much more productive and fun!

**Reinforcement and Bonuses:** This chapter has been Memory Optimized™ for your benefit. For your brief lesson and some great bonuses, visit www.planetfreedom .com/trainyourbrain with the access code on page 232. Enjoy!

# 12

# Top Tips for Supercharging Your Productivity

To wrap up this section on dealing with time, here's a smorgasbord of ideas for making yourself more productive. None of them are theories, all of them are strategies that I have personally gotten great results with and seen my clients get equally good results. You'll find that implementing even one or two of these strategies will make you much more effective with your time. Most of them will also help to turn on your subconscious mind to start making magic happen. So don't feel like you need to implement all of these tips immediately—rather pick one or two that you can get started with right away.

These are laid out in no particular order, except that #1 is definitely #1.

## Get Crystal Clear on Your Goals

I've heard it said that you'll never meet someone with a time management problem who doesn't also have a focus problem.

You've heard me say (in this book) that if you're not clear on what you want to accomplish, then how you manage your time is irrelevant. If you're looking for a way to boost your productivity, there's no question that the most impactful thing you can do is to simply have energizing goals. Remember all the great stuff you learned in the section on energizing goals? There's a reason why we covered it before the time usage section.

When you are clear on what you want to accomplish and why you want to accomplish it, you're just naturally more prone to things that work. You *automatically* heighten both your focus and your energy level, and it becomes much clearer how to prioritize your activities. When your goals fire you up, you will naturally guard your green time better, you will naturally attract more of the right people, the right ideas, and the right circumstances to help things move more quickly. The universe loves speed, and that speed is turned on by your mind being focused on and excited by your goals.

Having really energizing goals also makes you naturally *less* prone to what doesn't work. With energizing goals, you'll naturally be less prone to wasting time on TV, video games, and the Internet. You'll also notice that you'll have a force field that just steers negative interruptions away from you. When interruptions do happen (as they will), your goals will automatically make you deal with them more efficiently so they suck up less of your precious time.

When you have done the things that you learned in the "Have Energizing Goals" section of this book, you'll also automatically steer yourself away from the greatest time waster of all.

## Add by Subtraction

*The greatest waste of time is to do perfectly what needn't be done at all.* Not sure who said this first, but it's a quote I use all the time. Here's a good example of how cutting things out makes life better.

A while back my wife and kids were off on a little vacation, so I knew I'd have the entire weekend at my disposal. So what do you imagine I did? That's right, I worked on my yard! And I must say, I was stoked. For reasons I still can't fully understand, I couldn't have thought of a more enjoyable way to spend this time than cutting, mowing, pulling, mulching, and cleaning.

I wish I had taken before and after photos to show you what we're talking about, but suffice it to say that the place looked much better on Monday than it did on Friday. It almost wasn't the same home. Some of this was because of the mulch that got laid down to cover blemishes, some because my mom planted a few flowers, but most of the improvement came from the eight-foot high, 10-foot wide pile of branches, leaves, plants, and grass that simply got *eliminated*. The most effective improvement tools were the lawnmower, the pruning saw, and the hedge trimmer. The truly significant improvement came from what got *cut out*.

So what do you need to cut out?

What needs to be cut from your life? Some TV watching? Some snooze alarming? How about some operating without clear goals? Should you cut out starting the week without a plan? Are there any people you need to get away from so you can invest your time with a more inspiring crowd? Seriously, what patterns have you fallen into that would serve you best if you just took a scalpel to them?

At least as important as the to-do list is the stop-doing list—use it.

## The Daily Big Six

In Chapter 11, we strongly emphasized the practice of *weekly* planning, as opposed to the more common practice of a daily to-do list. This does not mean that you *shouldn't* plan out your day as well. The Two-Hour Solution gives context to a daily plan, and a daily plan puts teeth into the weekly. However, when it comes to creating a set of objectives for a single day, most people put too much on their lists, and/or they put items on it for the wrong reason.

The game is not to see how many things you can cross off a list, and it certainly isn't to see how many things you can put on. The game is to be as effective and productive as possible, so here's the absolute best method I've found. It's called the Daily Big Six, and I am shocked at how simple it is.

To mentally create a day, you only need to write down your answers to one question. The question is "What are the most impactful things I want to accomplish today?" You can answer however you like, and the only constraint is that you must limit yourself to a maximum of six answers for that day. Let me repeat that: no more than six significant objectives for any given day. If your answer is less than six, no problem. In fact, it's very common to have a Daily Big 3 or sometimes only a Daily Big 1. I promise you, if you write more than six, there are at least one or two things that simply aren't that important.

This method of approaching a day is actually so old that almost nobody even knows where it came from, but here's the value of this incredibly simple practice. The first known instance of it being taught was when an efficiency expert named Ivy Lee taught this technique to John D. Rockefeller in the early 1900s. Mr. Lee taught it to him and said, "Pay me whatever you believe this method to be worth." A few weeks later, Rockefeller sent him a check for $25,000 (in today's dollars that's over $500,000), along with a note explaining that he was still "drastically underpaying." When you shift the question from, "How many things can I cross off?" to "What are the six most important things I can accomplish?" your focus and your sense of urgency skyrocket. It makes the game a lot more fun.

### Organize at the End of the Day

Most people who implement the Two-Hour Solution and then the Daily Big Six will do their daily plan in the morning, before starting the day. This is certainly better than not doing it at all, but if you want to also crank up your subconscious mind to start working magic, do your Daily Big Six the night before. Sometime between wrapping up your workday and going to bed, take the few minutes you need to decide on your Daily Big Six for the next day.

This small difference does a couple of things that can put rocket fuel on your next day. First off, you'll go to sleep easier and wake up with more energy. Writing does something to settle things in your mind. So when you make the decision on your handful of most important objectives before going to bed, you remove some of the nagging questions that make it hard to rest. You also wake up without those questions and tend to hit the ground running in the morning. You'll learn more about how to maximize the first few minutes of your day in the Aggressive Mental Care section, but simply doing your Daily Big Six the night before can do wonders for getting your day off to a fast start.

Second, you actually flip your subconscious 180 degrees to start working for you while you sleep. Ever notice how if you have an argument or watch a stressful TV show right before falling asleep that it messes with your head? Crazy dreams, lots of tossing and turning, and so on? Guess what, you can make that tendency work for you just as easily as letting it work against you. Your brain is extremely active while you sleep, and it's doing some pretty big things. A lot of your brain's activity during sleep is to process what happened during the day, and then a lot of it is actually your subconscious getting you and your universe prepared for the next day. So by doing your Daily Big Six before bed, you actually plant thought seeds that your subconscious will go to work on while you're sleeping.

## Ramp up Your Self-Discipline

You may have noticed that a significant amount of this book is devoted to helping you get where you want to go in the most efficient manner possible. I am a huge believer in the idea of working smarter rather than harder . . . and I've also found that in many cases, working harder IS working smarter. Sometimes your success boils down to you simply making the decision that you're going to do whatever is necessary, for as long as necessary, to accomplish your goals and dreams. Back in the 30's, Albert Gray said that the Common Denominator of Success is that:

"Successful people form the habit of doing what unsuccessful people don't like to do."

A more modern translation comes from my friend Rory Vaden, author of the bestseller *Take The Stairs*. He calls it The Rent Axiom, and it's one of my all time favorites. He says that

"Success is never owned, it's rented—and the rent is due every day."

Oddly enough, when you make that commitment—that you're going to pay the rent every day—it frees up an enormous amount of energy and time. Make that commitment, and you become much more efficient and magnetic.

## For God's Sake, Stop Multitasking!!

Possibly the worst lie about time management is the one that says "If you can do more than one thing simultaneously, then clearly you can get more done in less time." That sounds like it should be true. I mean, just do the math, right? *Wrong!* Turns out that the more you try to do two things at once, let alone three or more, the worse your performance becomes, and ironically the longer it all takes. Don't buy it? Just google "multitasking research" and you'll find so much research on the phenomenon that it will make your head swim. I stopped looking after the twentieth article I read, because they all said the same three things:

1. Multitasking is a fallacy to begin with and people who think they're good at multitasking are totally lying to themselves.

According to Peter Bregman in the *Harvard Business Review*, doing several things at once is a trick we play on ourselves, thinking we're getting more done. In reality, our productivity goes down by as much as 40 percent. We don't actually multitask. We switch-task, rapidly shifting from one thing to another, interrupting ourselves unproductively, and losing time in the process.

2. Multitasking actually slows you down rather than speeding you up. According to Stanford University professor Anthony Wagner, "When they're in situations where there are multiple sources of information coming from the external world or emerging out of memory, [heavy multitaskers] are not able to filter out what's not relevant to their current goal.... That failure to filter means they're slowed down by that irrelevant information."

3. Multitasking doesn't just make you slower, it actually makes you stupider! "Multitasking adversely affects how you learn," said Russell Poldrack, UCLA associate professor of psychology. "Even if you learn while multitasking, that learning is less flexible and more specialized, so you cannot retrieve the information as easily." The effect of multitasking is literally a drop in your IQ equal to an entire sleepless night—approximately twice the effect of smoking marijuana.

Too many people wear their excellent ability to multitask as a badge of honor. What they are actually doing is lying to themselves while making themselves both slower and stupider. If that's you, knock it off.

### Work in Bursts, and Work during Primetimes

The antidote to the multitasking disease is to play to your brain's natural high-performance tendency: Work in bursts. You can focus intently on one thing for approximately 20 minutes at a time pretty easily, somewhat longer if what you're working on is important to you. After that, your brain just needs a break. So figure out a way to incorporate short breaks of three to five minutes into your day, once or twice per hour. Just simply stretching, taking a deep breath, or standing up for a brief period gives your brain the chance to hit the reset button in a way that keeps you productive and focused all day. In fact, that's how this book got written. The majority of the writing was done in a four-week stretch of time, and I did it about 25 minutes at a time. I've found that a day of work is best approached not as a marathon, but as a series of sprints.

The bonus tip in this area is to plan your bursts in accordance with your own natural primetimes. We all have a natural rhythm that our energy level follows. For example, I am a big-time early bird. I love being up before the sun, and I am highly motivated and creative at 5:30 in the morning. Some of my friends don't really get going until about 10 in the morning, and I know some people whose peak of energy happens somewhere around midnight. None of these are better or worse than another. If you can determine your natural energy high points, you can quite easily schedule the tasks that require your best thinking around those times.

## Guard Your Green Time

In Chapter 11, we discussed the concept of green time—time set aside for the activities that directly generate your living. I briefly mentioned that you should guard this time, and it's so important that it gets a whole tip here. You must guard and protect your green time aggressively, or it will get stolen from you. If your green time gets stolen, it literally means that your money is being stolen. Bill Zizzi, an early sales mentor of mine put it this way. He said, "When I'm selling, I make about $100 per hour. So if someone wastes half an hour of my time, they literally stole 50 bucks from me. I'm not going to just let that happen."

Of course nobody wants to let theft happen. If you aren't really mindful however, you will let green time get stolen from you. Who will steal it? You'll steal it from yourself. Why? The reason is that green time is often the toughest thing we have to do, so the two-year-old part of our brain can do a great job of finding excuses. For a salesperson, prospecting is emotionally challenging, so it's easy to somehow make "research" a higher priority. For a student, actually doing the science project is hard, so it becomes easy to just put it off one more day. For an executive, delivering a necessary piece of bad news is not fun, so their brains will come up with all kinds other projects to take precedence. Do not confuse activity with accomplishment—you're literally taking money out of your own pocket.

### Schedule Interruptions (huh?)

When it's not you that's stealing green time from you, it certainly can be other people. Remember Quadrant 3, the quadrant of deceit? Other people will unquestionably steal a lot of time from you if you let them. Especially if you work from home, it often seems like people just think that you must not be doing much of anything! Don't get mad about it, just learn to deal. Two ways:

*Proactively*: When you do your weekly Two-Hour Solution, make sure to communicate your schedule to two groups of people—the people who mean the most to you and the people who most often interrupt you. My wife and I both do our own version of the Two-Hour Solution independently, and then we come together to mesh up our schedules (communication is key). For people I work with, my schedule gets shared on Google Calendar so they can see when it's okay to call me and when it's not.

*Responsively*: Even if people know when your "office hours" are, they will still show up and say, "Hey can you help me with _____ right now?" This instance is where the magic of flex time shows up. First off you must be firm and at least attempt to schedule an appointment to help this person with whatever he or she needs. Direct them to the fact that you have a schedule that you've thought through, and point out that you've actually set aside time to deal with situations like theirs—three hours here, an hour there, another significant block somewhere else. Often, they will simply deal with their own issue (usually a win for both of you); sometimes it will be important and they will in fact schedule an appointment (also a win for both of you). In the rare instance where you really do need to drop what you are doing, you still win, because you've set up Flex Time for yourself! You must, however, begin training people that you have a plan. It'll be tough at first, but you'll notice after about three weeks that the number of interruptions and distractions in your life has dropped considerably.

## Set Boundaries on Technology

The last time thief is technology, specifically communications technology. Cell phone, text messaging, and e-mail can steal so much time and energy it's criminal, and it's not necessary. My friend Tom Weber says it best. Tom is big time into Facebook, Twitter, texting and social media, but his philosophy is that those technologies exist for him to communicate with clients and loved ones when he wants, not for them to have access to him all the time that they want. So just decide ahead of time when you'll respond to texts, e-mails, and voicemails and let people know. For me there's a lot of time each day where I am simply unavailable to anyone. If I'm speaking, coaching, or in a meeting, my phone is off. When I'm with my family, I choose to be with them fully. And sometimes I just know that I won't want to talk to anyone for a morning or an afternoon. So my outgoing voicemail changes every day to let people know when I will return calls, and nobody ever gets upset when they can't reach me immediately. E-mail autoresponders can accomplish the same thing. It's a two-minute investment each day that pays huge dividends in my own focus as well as my credibility with people who are important.

Believe me, there's nothing in business that can't wait for four hours. The things that are really important are never that urgent. Set boundaries and enforce them lovingly—you'll be glad you did.

## Take Advantage of Parkinson's Law

Have you ever noticed how you become über-productive right before a vacation? That happens to nearly everyone, and it's no coincidence. This is partly because having something to look forward to just boosts your enthusiasm, and it's partly because of an amazing principle called Parkinson's Law. Parkinson's Law states that: *"Work expands so as to fill the time available for its completion."* My clients have noticed that work will also *contract* so as to fill the time available for its completion. Give yourself more time, tasks will take you longer. Give yourself less time, and it's amazing how the same task will usually get done, with the same or better quality. Few things spark energy and productivity like a hard deadline.

I mentioned earlier my client Roger, who owns a catering business. He gave me a great example of how if his staff usually has six hours to prep a catering job, they will always finish in exactly six hours. Often, however, circumstances dictate that they only have four hours to prep the exact same job, and they finish in exactly four hours. Surprisingly (or not), the work they do in four hours is usually better than the work they do in six, and the staff actually enjoys it more. There's more energy, more spark, more enthusiasm—the four-hour job is just higher quality in every way possible.

So how to take advantage of this?

Compress deadlines. Try giving yourself less time than you think you need. If it normally takes you two hours to write a particular report, try starting an hour before the end of your day. You'll finish in an hour, you'll do great work, and you'll be amazed at how you found an extra hour every time you have to do that report again. If your sales presentation normally takes, say, 30 minutes, set an alarm for 20 and when it goes off you must close. My fifth year in sales I doubled my income largely because of this one technique.

For enhancing both quantity and quality of production in a given time frame, I've found very few tips that work better than compressing deadlines and letting Parkinson's Law work for me, rather than against me.

## Become a Spectacular Listener

Okay, here's one that you probably never thought of as a productivity tip: Become a great listener. I am shocked by how much time gets wasted simply because we don't truly hear what someone is saying. Remember the greatest time waster of all—doing perfectly what needn't be done at all. When this happens it is often done with the best intentions. We really want to help our spouse, our friend, or our client, and we kill ourselves doing something for them that they didn't really want in the first place.

One of my clients is a sales manager for a water treatment company, and he described to me how he had a meeting with a prospect, convinced that he knew what they needed before even showing up. As a result, he didn't listen super well, didn't ask very many or very good questions, and left the meeting convinced he really did know what they wanted. So he literally spent days putting together a proposal based on what he projected mentally onto them and on what he thought he heard.

And he was fired up to deliver this proposal. Fortunately for him, he never got to deliver it. In his extensive research, he needed to call the client with a minor question, and that conversation—the one where he was actually listening with both ears open and his mouth mostly closed—led to a conversation where he realized the entire premise of his proposal was almost the total opposite of what this customer actually wanted and needed. This was both unfortunate and very fortunate. Unfortunate in the sense that he had to start all over again (mostly wasted a couple of days), fortunate in the sense that (his words), "If I would have delivered my original proposal, not only would I have completely wasted the time, I actually would have alienated this particular customer and probably lost them." Which would have led to a much longer amount of time prospecting for new business to replace this customer.

Great listening is a great time saver. The subject of effective listening is likely to be another entire book, so for starters apply these three concepts:

1. If you don't understand a question, keep clarifying until you do.

2. Once you think you understand someone, don't move on until you've confirmed with them by explaining what they said back to them.

3. God gave you two ears and one mouth—use them proportionately.

There you are—12 tips that, used in conjunction with the Two-Hour Solution will make your time a lot more productive and keep your energy and focus high. Enjoy!

**Reinforcement and Bonuses:** This chapter has been Memory Optimized™ for your benefit. For your brief lesson and some great bonuses, visit www.planetfreedom.com/trainyourbrain with the access code on page 232. Enjoy!

# Component #3
# Be Brilliant with the Basics

*The most important part of the ...*
*process is the ... person.*

Zig Ziglar

# 13

# The Basics of You Part 1: Your Personal Core Values

---

*I would not give a fig for the simplicity this side of complexity, but I would give my life for the simplicity on the other side of complexity.*
—Oliver Wendell Holmes

Thus far all of *Train Your Brain for Success* has been devoted to skills and techniques. Which is terrific, because we all need skills and techniques for thriving in our world. Even taken in a vacuum, the tips you've gotten here for improving your memory, your reading ability, your goal setting, and how you deal with your time will definitely help your life work better than it does without them. Yes, we all need to know *what to do*. Most people don't even know that, and you can break records just by being exceptional on that level.

If you're like most of our clients, however, you may have noticed that if all you're ever working on is the how-to, you'll eventually find yourself wanting more. It's very likely that you have tried some type of goal-setting/time-management/self-improvement plan before. In fact, as a reader of a book like this I'd be a little surprised if you hadn't. As such you've proba-bly had the experience of getting all fired up for your new system, but after somewhere between three days and three weeks you hit a wall. You either got frustrated with a technique, you found that no matter how hard you tried you weren't quite getting there, or for some reason you ended up asking the question, "What am I doing all of this for anyhow?" You needed context, you needed to understand your *why*.

It's been said that if your *why* is big enough, then the *how* will tend to take care of itself, and I've found that to be true in every area of life. When you can answer the big questions—

Why am I here?

What is my life really all about?

—then all of the how-to stuff becomes much richer. So in the next two chapters, you're going to spend some time walking down the path of determining these answers for yourself. In this chapter we'll walk through one of the first homework assignments I give my coaching clients on discovering your personal core values. In Chapter 14 we'll help you get clear on a purpose and vision. When you have those in place, you set yourself on a firm foundation for your growth. I will warn you that doing this right takes some time, but it's so worth it. If you'll take the time to answer the questions and do the exercises in these next few chapters, you'll come out with a significantly stronger platform for understanding of why all of this stuff is important to you in the first place, and in the process you'll actually become much clearer on who you are.

## A Structured Way of Answering the Big Question "What Is My Life Really About?"

The question "What is my life about?" is a doozy. I mean really, it's one of those that college kids like to sit up all night gazing at the stars and philosophizing about, right? It's so big that most people never get any answers to it. For some, they shy away from taking the time to think about it. For others it kind of runs around in the back of the mind constantly, nagging like a mosquito. Either way, the question often seems too big to answer, so we never actually sit down and address it. Let's make it a little easier:

First off, we're not asking the question "What's life all about?" You're asking yourself "What's *your* life all about?" These are *your* answers. There is no possibility of having better or worse answers than anyone else, because you are the only one who can really answer the question for yourself.

Second, we've actually developed, and for 10 years taught, a way of thinking through this question in a way that actually produces some solid answers. Let's discover your Personal Core Values.

## What's a Core Value?

In business circles, you hear a lot of talk about "core values" for companies—it's another one of those things that's become a bit of a buzzword. So you'll notice that many companies have a plaque with their core values posted near the front door. Some companies really live out those values and for some it's lip service (and you can usually tell). Regardless of how businesses handle the issue, when core values are discovered on an individual level, it's one of the most powerful and permanent anchors you can develop for your life. Your personal core values are simply the handful of principles, ideas, or concepts that you want your life to be about.

Here are some good questions to stimulate and guide your thinking on this issue.

- When people see your life, what do you want them to see?
- What do you want your life to represent, when you are at your best?

- If someone were speaking about you at an awards banquet, what would you want them to say about you?
- If someone were speaking about you at your funeral, what would you want them to say your life was all about?

What you're going to do is get down on paper, in your own words, the handful of principles, ideas, and concepts that truly inspire you—that you want your life to be about. I'll walk you through the exercise I do with my clients and with myself every few years. Once you've done the process, I'll show you what came out the other end for me.

## Where Do I Start?

Here's a great way of figuring out what ideas, principles, or concepts inspire you the most. This is actually an interactive exercise, so you'll need a pen or highlighter for this, and some scratch paper as well. Look over the following list of words. Hear each one in your mind and feel it in your heart. Some of these will resonate with you and some not so much. Look over this list and circle or highlight every one that does something for you. As you're doing this exercise, it's pretty common for words to come to mind that are not on the list but really do it for you. If you have that experience, definitely write those words down. Understand that none of these words are better or worse than any other. Approach this exercise without judgment and with an open mind, and just notice which of these words inspire you. Ready, set, go.

| | |
|---|---|
| Integrity | Prosperity |
| Love | Family |
| Peace | Excitement |
| Growth | Security |
| Joy | Community |
| Health | Change |

Toughness

Happiness

Fun

Wealth

Freedom

Transformation

Power

Unity

Harmony

Physical Fitness

Adventure

Stability

Excellence

Peace of Mind

Patience

Children

Legacy

Abundance

Nature

Acceptance

Strength

Speed

Education

Knowledge

Wisdom

Honesty

Contentment

Gratitude

Enthusiasm

Humor

Spirituality

Learning

Laughter

Purity

Friendship

Discipline

Hard Work

Leisure

Individuality

Creativity

Spontaneity

Longevity

Competition

Energy

Being Rich

Being Poor

Communication

Giving

Kindness

Self Control

Choice

Equality

Experimentation

Grace

Compassion

Sincerity

Approval

Attractiveness

Partnership

Winning

Truth

Intelligence

Neatness

Comfort

Faith

Achievement

Innovation

Beauty

Flexibility

Structure

Mastery

Leadership

Openness

Clarity

Diversity

People

Depth

Lightness

Courage

Vision

Belief

Passion

Justice

Relationship

Exploration

Quality

Luxury

Loyalty

Risk

Goodness

Balance

Authenticity

Hope

Trust

Influence

How many did you identify? There are 115 words on that list. My guess is that your number is somewhere between 15 and 30. Great start! Take all of those and write them on a separate sheet of paper right now.

## How Do I Narrow It Down?

As I said before, your brain can only deal effectively with five to seven things at a time, and your core values follow this pattern as well. In counseling thousands of people on this, I've never seen anyone have a list of more than 7 values *where they weren't repeating themselves*. Your job is to take the couple of dozen you have in front of you and narrow them down to a handful. A handful means somewhere between four and seven. So yes, you'll need to make some decisions here. Here are two tips for making this as easy as possible:

#1. You'll notice that you probably have clusters of words picked out that are pretty similar, or potentially mean kind of the same thing to you. You'll likely spot combinations that look like "Faith/Spirituality/Compassion," or "Humor/Joy/Laughter/Enthusiasm," and so on. So group those together. Once you notice your clusters, it's your job to decide what you really mean. Sometimes when you group the words in this way, one of them really jumps out as the best descriptor of that concept. Sometimes you look at all of them and think, "None of them individually are the real deal for me, but when I add them all up I get _____" (some other word that wasn't even on the original list but is the right term for you).

#2. Understand that the words you take off your list are not lost forever. Sometimes when our clients do this exercise they struggle with feeling like they are choosing one child over another! The words that you don't choose as the primary core value term will often show up to be used in the next step—your definitions. So don't worry, you can use them all eventually, but you do need to narrow it down. Again, what you're looking for are five to seven words that really ring your bell and make you say, "Yeah, that's what *I'm all about.*"

(Note: If you are stuck, please reach out to me and my staff. At Freedom Personal Development, we literally take our clients by the hand and coach them through this process of discovering personal core values, sometimes over a period of weeks. It's some of the best work we do. )

### Decide on Your Definitions

Once you've got the list down to a handful of words, it's time to answer the question, "What does that mean to *you*?" In this step, there is no right or wrong, only what you find to be true and inspiring for you. If your core values are to have the power to inspire your daily decisions about how you live your life, you must decide on the definition of your terms.

For example, the word "integrity" is the one that shows up most frequently on our clients' lists, but I've seen it defined in many different ways. For some, integrity means simply telling the truth. For some it contains an element of solidity or strength, as in the structural integrity of a building. For some, "integrity" is the same as "loyalty." Others have totally different definitions. How you define a core value doesn't matter, except that it really matters that you have defined it for yourself.

Again, if the practice of defining these abstract terms is challenging, don't hesitate to get some help. Two tools my clients and I have found to be incredibly valuable are:

#1. A dictionary—Often just seeing what Noah Webster had to say about a word is really helpful.

#2. A coach—Once again, this is an area where you may want to reach out to me or my staff. I've found that many people just have very little practice in expressing the meaning of core values terms. Having a knowledgable and caring person ask you good questions about what you mean and then offer some help with wordsmithing can be incredibly valuable for getting at the essence of what you're really trying to say.

Get out your scratch paper or your computer, and write out your definitions—enjoy!

### Rank 'em.

Last step here: Decide on what order they belong in. It's rare that you'll ever have to choose between your core values, but maybe not as rare as you might think. Here's an example:

One of the things that has allowed my company, Freedom Personal Development, to flourish is that before we decided what we wanted to sell and how we wanted to sell it, we got extremely clear on our organization's core values. We literally locked ourselves in a room for three days straight and lobbied, argued and discussed until we came out with our original set of five core values: Integrity, Joy, Freedom, Excellence, and Profitability, in that order. The reason we needed to determine the ranking is that we knew we'd have decisions to make where any decision would cause us to favor one core value over another. Integrity versus profitability is common in any business, and ours is no exception. Would we have the opportunity to cut corners and maybe underdeliver sometimes to squeeze a little more profit out of a client or a workshop? Of course we would have those opportunities. Having a clear and published set of core values that guide our decisions gives us a standard of accountability that makes it very obvious which way to go. Having them ranked makes us much more likely to actually live out those values in the moment of truth.

It works the same way in your life. In your moments of truth which way do you go? Sadly, when confronted with the realities of life many people end up going in a direction they really would not prefer. A survey was taken of parents about what they considered most important in their choice of breakfast foods for their kids—specifically, breakfast cereal. Overwhelmingly, the answer from the survey was "*nutrition*." If you look at the top 10 *selling* breakfast cereals however, let's just say that you don't see the value of nutrition represented anywhere near as strongly as the survey answers should indicate. When confronted with reality, what people *say* versus what they *do* is important, and the two are often very different. My observation is that much of this stems from the fact that most people have never really thought through what's most important to them. They've never given themselves the compass that clearly identified, defined, and ordered core values provide. This saying versus doing discrepancy causes a tremendous amount of turbulence and commotion in your subconscious, which drains energy and undermines self-esteem to a degree that is difficult to overstate. Fortunately, much of this turbulence will be remedied if you'll simply walk through the exercise I've just described. Will it take some time? Yes. Is it worth it? Unquestionably.

## What Do I Do with the Results?

The final step with your core values is to put your ranked definitions into one place, and then place them in one or more locations where you will be able to see them. Start off by getting them off your scratch paper and placing them here:

Core Value #1: _____
Definition:

_____
_____
_____
_____
_____
_____
_____

Core Value #2: _____
Definition:

_____
_____
_____
_____
_____
_____
_____
_____

Core Value #3: _____
Definition:

_____
_____
_____
_____
_____
_____
_____
_____
_____

Core Value #4: _____
Definition:

_____
_____
_____
_____
_____
_____
_____
_____
_____

Core Value #5: _____
Definition:

_____
_____
_____
_____
_____
_____
_____
_____
_____

Core Value #6: _____
Definition:

_____
_____
_____
_____
_____
_____
_____
_____

Core Value #7: _____
Definition:

_____
_____
_____
_____
_____
_____
_____
_____

Once you've got them all together I strongly recommend making several copies and making them part of your daily life. I wanted to include my own personal document here for the sake of example. You shouldn't copy these (unless they really do work for you); I just thought it might be helpful for you to see a completed example that works really well. I was recently coaching a group of clients through this process of identifying, defining, and ranking their personal core values and realized that I hadn't mindfully done this for myself in several years. Core values can change as priorities and life situations change over a period of many years, so I re-did mine in 2011 and it came out like this:

## My Core Values

**Integrity**

Doing what's right and doing what's necessary, even when I don't feel like it and even when nobody is looking. Living with integrity requires discipline and breeds peace of mind.

**Joy**

Making the choice to be positive, enthusiastic, and upbeat with a humorous perspective, whether circumstances warrant it or not.

**Excellence**

Continuously improving the effectiveness of my performance, and by extension the quality of my life. Living a life of excellence is the key to being an inspiration.

**Abundance**

The knowing that there is way more of everything than we need, in every area of life. Focusing on abundance produces gratitude and makes me magnetically attractive.

**Freedom**

The capacity to exercise choice. The better steward I am of my freedom, the more my freedom grows, and the better life gets!

This document lives on the desktop of my computer, and I review it daily during my Power Hour (you'll learn about it in the section on Aggressive Mental Care). I also have a printed copy that lives in my office, one in my car, and one in my

Quarterly Goals notebook. I've seen people place copies on their refrigerator, on the ceiling above their bed, on a vision board as an anchor, and so on. There are innumerable places that would be appropriate to make your core values visible—you pick yours and let them saturate your vision and your mind. You'll notice yourself making different and better decisions. When you make decisions that don't honor your core values, you at least become aware of the discrepancy. This moves you to do it differently next time. Over time, you literally train your subconscious to favor the choices that embody your core values over those that don't. It's a profound change, and I encourage you to enjoy it.

**Reinforcement and Bonuses:** This chapter has been Memory Optimized™ for your benefit. For your brief lesson and some great bonuses, visit www.planetfreedom .com/trainyourbrain with the access code on page 232. Enjoy!

# 14

# The Basics of You Part 2: Purpose and Vision

## Be, Do, Have

The most fundamental model of how we create results in our world is called **Be, Do, Have**. It means that the person you are—your character and your thinking—lays the foundation and gives the flavor to all the things you do. What you do then is the direct creator of your results: the *have*. This is the seed of a lot of well-known personal development quotes such as these:

*If you think you can or you think you can't—either way you're right. It's the thinking that makes it so.*

—Henry Ford

*What the mind of man can conceive and believe, it can achieve.*

—Napoleon Hill

And numerous others. There are so many ways of under-standing and learning from this model that it's probably an entire book unto itself. The primary lesson to get here is that the clearer and more aligned you are between your Be and your *Do*, the easier and more naturally you will *Have* the results you are looking for.

# A Structured Way of Answering the Other Big Question: What Do I Want to **Do**?

Chapter 13 helped you address the big question, "What's my life all about?" If you took the time to walk through the exercise we did there, you really went a long way toward getting a handle on the *Be* component of Be, Do, Have. Well, guess what—If you don't translate your values into action, you miss out. You don't impact the world; you don't make your values live. You also don't get tangible results. It's not just Be... Have. It's Be, **Do**, Have. True, Napoleon Hill didn't write Act and Grow Rich, he wrote *Think and Grow Rich*, but if you've read that masterpiece you'll find that the entire work is infused with specific things to *do*. Action is ultimately what directly leads to every result in your life. It's been said that "if you do the right things the right way, and do them consistently for a long enough time, you will get results." Be is the foundation of action, Have is a by-product of action; Do is where the rubber meets the road.

At Freedom Personal Development we often find our coach-ing clients failing in the area of taking the right actions, in two ways.

## Acting Out of Context

Our coaching clients never come to us out of laziness. Most of our coaching clients are pretty successful to begin with, usually very goal-oriented and hard-working. And they've literally been working their brains out for years. They act, act, act, and the result is that they've achieved (in many cases achieved well), but they are exhausted. Can you relate?

This happens because all that action is happening out of context. It's producing results, but the question of "Why am I doing this?" has never been answered. Again, it's such a big question that we try to avoid it altogether. But we can't avoid it entirely, because your brain wants to know why—it needs it. So what happens is that we get fleeting thoughts floating through our minds like:

- "Where is all of this going?"
- "What am I doing with my life?"
- "Is this really what I was meant to do?"
- "What's the point here?"

If this is happening, even successful results can be somewhat unfulfilling. The other problem with massive action out of context is that it's really exhausting. More energy than we realize goes to those questions, and when they remain unresolved they exert a significant drain.

## No Action at All Due to Paralysis

The other action related issue we see a lot is the issue of paralysis. When people don't have the answer to the why question, the brain's tendency is to not do anything at all. It goes back to the issue of the comfort zone—where you are hasn't killed you yet, so your brain will default to staying there, unless something moves or inspires it.

This issue results not so much in exhaustion, but in feeling like you're stuck. You know you should be doing something, but you're just unable to get off the dime and move forward. Have you ever felt this way?

## Killing Two Birds with One Stone

Fortunately, both the exhaustion of acting out of context and the stuck-ness of being paralyzed can be alleviated by actually developing *your own* concise answer to the question, "What is the purpose of my life?" and then crystalizing that into *your own* long-range mental image of how that purpose plays out. That's what we're going to do with the rest of this chapter.

This is a deceptively simple process—simple as in it's literally a fill-in-the blank exercise followed by one question, deceptive in that coming up with answers that really satisfy you may take a fair amount of time. It may also challenge your thinking a bit, so be prepared to focus here.

## Your Purpose Statement

There are a lot of ways of asking and answering the question "What's my purpose?". What our clients and I have found to be the most effective way for an individual to ask and answer it is what follows. To give credit where credit is due, I or we did not invent this question. In the late 1990s my friend Eric Plantenberg and I read a little-known book by Kevin McCarthy called *The On-Purpose Business*, which we learned later was actually a follow up to his book, *The On-Purpose Person*. The almost ridiculously simple exercise at the center of both books hit us both right between the eyes, and has revolutionized the thinking of tens of thousands since.

If you want to figure out what you're here for, here's how to create a purpose statement. Just fill in the blanks of the following statement in the way that:

a. makes sense to you.

b. really inspires you.

I exist to serve by _____ing _____.

That's it—just fill in the blanks. There are just a few guidelines. The first blank gets filled in with a verb, an action word. The second blank gets filled in with a noun—a person, place, or thing (in this instance the "thing" would probably be an idea or a concept) or possibly an adjective—a descriptive word. Again, to be complete, your answer must

a. Make sense to *you*.
b. Really inspire *you*.

Much like the core values exercise, no answer is better or worse than another, as long as they meet the criteria. My only other recommendation on your answers is that they should not depend on anyone else; your answers should be your answers regardless of what anyone else does. It's your own purpose statement and should be insulated. More on this concept in a bit.

### My Purpose Statement Story

I will confess that when I first did this exercise I was blessed with a bit of a lightning bolt. It's entirely possible that may happen for you; in fact it may have already happened. Eric actually was reading *The On-Purpose Business*, and while we were out for a run he hit me with the fill-in-the-blank exercise. Cruising along, it only took a few seconds for me. The first answer that came into my mind felt perfect and has stayed with me for more than a decade. For me the answer was

"I exist to serve by *bringing joy*."

That resonated with me, and the more I thought about it the more it made sense. The noun "joy" was already a core value for me and the definition was very clear in my mind. This is actually why we teach core values before purpose, as one of those is likely to be your noun. The verb "*bringing*" meant that it was my responsibility to just bring joy to every situation. Other people taking some joy was the desired result, but not necessary for me to be living my purpose. For me these thoughts came very quickly, and I feel lucky that they did. If that's happened for you, great! Take whatever came to you and write it down. Let it marinate for a little while, come back to it, and just let it sink in.

### *Your Purpose Statement Story*

If you're like a lot of our clients, you didn't get hit with the lightning bolt as I did—no problem. You'll just need to consider your answers and wrestle with them until you come out with something that works for you. This is another area (much like discovering your core values) where a coach can be incredibly helpful. Our 12-week P.A.C.T (Personal Accountability Training and Coaching) program has the first third of it devoted to just working through the issues we're discussing in this section on "The Basics of You"—yes, that's four weeks. So don't be discouraged if you could use some outside perspective on this. Keep at it until you get the answers you need, and please get some guidance if you could use it.

As an assist here, take a look at some examples that my clients have arrived at:

"I exist to serve by creating growth."
"I exist to serve by teaching life's lessons."
"I exist to serve by being real."
"I exist to serve by expanding horizons."

All of these are actual purpose statements that my associates or clients have developed with a little help. Notice that they all fit the structure, and I can tell you from being there for the creation of these statements that they truly resonate with the individuals that created them. None is better or worse than another. We each have a unique aspect to our purpose, and your purpose statement should reflect you.

The only precaution I'll give is that your purpose statement must not be dependent on circumstance. Also, it definitely must not be dependent on the behavior or thinking of anyone else. This is what I mean by "insulated." I can "bring joy" everywhere all the time, no matter what. My client Ernie Curley can "teach life's lessons" everywhere all the time, no matter what. Eric

Plantenberg could "be real" always and everywhere. Yes, the existence of the word "*serve*" in the statement implies that your purpose is to impact the world somehow, but it's key for your purpose statement that the participation of other people is not required. You must be insulated from that burden.

I say this because I've seen purpose statements backfire when the approval or participation of others is required. I think of one individual who came up with "I exist to serve by inspiring others". This sounded really cool and fit the structure, but do you see how this person was set up to fail? The problem with this particular statement is that if somebody happened to *not* be inspired by my friend, which could happen for an infinite number of reasons beyond her control, then she would be *failing to live out her purpose*. She would have been giving control of her life's purpose to people she didn't know, and that is dangerous for the spirit. You want to be able to live out your purpose statement in *every possible situation*, even when you are alone or when other people choose not to participate.

I strongly encourage you to take whatever time is necessary to craft your purpose statement before moving on. If your *why* is big enough, the *how* will take care of itself. Give yourself that foundation for action.

## Your Vision Statement

We've talked about how your mind thinks in images. The fundamental way that your subconscious creates your results and your life is that it *sees images and moves toward them*. We discussed this earlier, when you learned about my friend Dave teaching his daughter how to ride her bike without training wheels. Remember? "Don't run into the telephone pole!" versus "Ride straight toward me!" produces a very different result.

The importance of having a vision for your life is the final piece of the basics of you, and its value cannot be overstated.

Without a clear vision for where you want your life to go, it becomes easy to spin your wheels or wander. In *Alice in Wonderland*, I love this dialogue between the Cheshire Cat and Alice, as she stops to ask him for directions:

Cat: "Where would you like to go?"
Alice: "I don't really know..."
Cat: "In that case, any road will get you there."

The Bible puts it a little more directly: "Without vision, the people perish." Get that fully—the people don't just "suffer" or "become uncomfortable"—they *die*. Aristotle was among the first to state that human beings are *teleological*, meaning that we are inherently designed to be working toward something. When we aren't, we start to stagnate and die. Without a clear vision for where we want to go, we literally drain our own life energy and we hasten our death, literally and figuratively.

However, when we do have a vision, we become instantly successful. Earl Nightingale defined success as "the progressive realization of a worthy ideal." The key words in that definition are progressive and worthy. Progressive means that it's about being on the path—any progress towards a worthy ideal is success. A worthy ideal means that you are working toward some ideal or goal that you believe to be worthy. Life is not about having a big house, a fancy car, a lot of money, or cool toys. Life is about moving toward something that you are passionate and enthusiastic about. It's not about "Did you get there yet?" It's about "Are you getting there?"

Some good news is that your vision doesn't need to be perfect for it to work for you. I'll show you how to craft one here shortly, so understand that even an incomplete or imperfect vision statement is much more effective than none at all. I mean, I'm constantly working to refine and update mine. Mine is a living document, and I encourage you to make yours into one as well. In its ideal manifestation, a personal vision statement becomes a *skopos*. I first heard this word in a sermon preached by Alex Gee in 1994, and it was definitely the best sermon I ever heard. I hope I can do the concept justice. *Skopos* is the Greek word for goal, but it implies much more than that. It implies vision—it's the root word for our modern word *scope*. If you think about the word scope, it essentially means everything that you can see. It shows up in words like telescope and microscope.

So it's one thing to have a goal, but it's a whole different ballgame to have a *skopos*. As Pastor Gee said, "When you get a vision it might be in your eyes. But when you get a skopos, it's in your feet. When you get a skopos, your feet move towards it. When you get a skopos, your hands move toward it." And then eventually, you don't have to push yourself anymore, because your vision drags you into it and pulls you along. A real, true, powerful vision for your life will cause you to go to the place where motivation is no longer necessary because it just burns from within you. And my friend, when you are on fire with a skopos, people will come from all around just to watch you burn. It's the real deal.

Throughout history, people have been given visions—Joan of Arc, Henry Ford, Andrew Carnegie, Moses, Muhammad. But you don't need to wait for a miracle—you owe it to yourself to help the process along. You can give your own life skopos that it really wants.

Here's how we do it.

### Constructing Your Personal Vision Statement

Again, this process is deceptively simple. You just answer a simple question, in a way that gets your juices flowing when you read it.

The question is:

"In the next five to seven years, what do you want your life to look like?"

That's the gist. If you had the opportunity to wave your magic wand and create the ideal life for yourself (which you actually do, as long as you're willing to wave that wand called your thinking and then get to work), what would that life look like? When you have a written answer that gets you going, you have an effective personal vision statement.

A couple of guidelines:

1. Note the time frame suggested—five to seven years. This is not set in stone. When you craft a personal vision statement, understand that you are mentally creating your ideal life. If it really is your ideal life, who cares if it takes five years versus seven or ten? The whole point is the image itself, so don't get hung up on the time frame.

2. I recommend answering this question for each area of your life. Professional, financial, physical, family, community/social, and mental/emotional/spiritual each get their own vision statement. The example you'll see below is the vision statement I created for the professional area of my life in 2010.

3. Your answer should definitely have subjective qualities to it; not all of it needs to be specific and measurable. I also recommend that your answer have some objective qualities, like numbers and statistics. You'll see both qualities in the example below.

4. Your answer should be written in the present tense, as if it is happening right now. Phrases like "I am," "we are," "our clients love," "my family experiences," and the like are actual images that your mind can see. This is much more powerful than something written in the future tense. "I'm going to," "we will," "our clients will love," or "my family wants to experience" will not create as much. You'll notice in the example below that the present tense is used throughout.

So here's an example of what an effective personal vision statement can look like:

---

## My Professional Vision

Freedom Personal Development has become the world's premier personal development company. In terms of numbers, the company does $20,000,000 in annual sales, with exactly the right number of speakers and bookers generating that revenue, along with a kick-ass marketing system that generates results 24/7. Inside salespeople have a clear path to at least $100,000/year income, while speakers make an average of at least $250,000. Our total staff is a group of happy, hard-working people. We love what we do, we do it to the highest level of excellence and integrity, and each individual earns an income that they are ecstatic about.

Our clients experience a series of life-changing workshops, coaching programs, audio/video resources, and books. Between our entry point workshops like Memory Training and Reading Smart (and more to come), our weekend events, our advanced retreats like the Abundant Living Retreat (and more to come), our personal coaching programs, and our home study resources, our clients have the ability and the desire to develop true lifetime partnerships with us. I personally bring value to tens of thousands each year as a leader, a coach, an author, and a teacher. I deliver 35 to 40 fee-paid programs per year, and I never need to leave town for less than $10,000. My working time is devoted to these things:

- Creating resources for our clients to purchase and benefit from (writing and recording).

*(continued)*

---

(*continued*)

- Delivering keynotes and workshops worldwide to groups of all sizes and getting paid handsomely for it. Getting me in front of a group is expensive and totally worth it.

- Coaching leaders, internally at FPD and externally at our client companies. One-on-one time with me is expensive and totally worth it.

- Architecting and leading FPD on its path to being the world's premier personal development firm.

The result of this is that I have a million-dollar business inside of FPD. This helps to serve as the template for everyone in our company to build the same level of success (or better).

My time is under my control. I am intensely present, focused, and productive when working, and I take six to eight weeks of vacation every year with zero guilt and zero negative effect on our company. In short, I am passionate about what I do and it creates enthusiasm, energy, joy, and abundance for me and for those surrounding me.

For some additional questions to stimulate your thinking, check out the "Reinforcement and Bonus" section at the end of this chapter.

## What Do I Do with This, Now That It's Crafted?

Once you have a personal vision statement crafted, I recommend you do these things with it.

1. Spend time with it on a daily basis. In Chapter 17, you'll see that part of the daily energy management practice we teach involves reading your personal vision statement. So make it part of your Power Hour. Barring that, make absolutely certain that the first step of your Two-Hour Solution involves you reading and seeing your personal vision statement. That way you're reviewing it at least weekly.

2. Make it a living document. Don't allow this to become static. Once it's done, other ideas likely will come to you. You may feel a desire to add to the statement—go for it!

3. To balance #2, don't regularly make wholesale changes. There are only two times when it's appropriate to just throw the whole thing out and start over. One is if your life undergoes a significant change and you find that your original vision just isn't meaningful for you. The other is when you actually realize your vision.

If you haven't already taken the time to craft your personal vision statement, get going now. If you really get stuck, reach out to me and my staff. We can help you get moving again.

**Reinforcement and Bonuses:** This chapter has been Memory Optimized™ for your benefit. For your brief lesson and some great bonuses, visit www.planetfreedom .com/trainyourbrain with the access code on page 232. Enjoy!

# Record-Breaking Component #4
# Aggressive Mental Care

# 15

# The Most Basic Piece: Energy

The fourth component of a record-breaking performance is practicing Aggressive Mental Care. As we studied top achievers and those that were breaking records, one of the strongest (and least surprising) tendencies we noticed was that these individuals and organizations systematically take excellent care of their minds. They proactively put positive thoughts into their mind and kept negative ones out. A little more in-depth study taught me why this is so important.

It has to do with the Second Law of Thermodynamics. "What? I've never heard of the Second Law of Thermodynamics —what are you talking about, Roger?" Hang in there, this is interesting and applicable.

We can all agree that if you are to break records in any area of your life, that it will require a high level of energy, right? Even outside of the context of what we're covering here in *Train Your Brain For Success*, there's almost nobody who wouldn't like to have more energy in their body and/or their life. It just makes sense—you can't get high-powered results without high power!

Well, if you want more energy, an understanding of the Second Law of Thermodynamics is actually critical, because it affects every energy system in the universe—and you, my friend, are an energy system in it's purest form!

Thermodynamics as a branch of science is simply the study of how energy moves. The First Law of Thermodynamics you've probably heard—it's the one that states that "energy can be neither created nor destroyed, it can only change form." That's interesting in and of itself, but the Second Law applies directly to your own energy level. It states that (I'm paraphrasing here) in any energy system—from a plant to a car to a house to your body to the entire universe—that the transfer of energy is never 100 percent efficient; there is always some level of "energy leakage." This energy leakage leads to a higher and higher level of disorganization or chaos (known as entropy) in that system. In fact, the Second Law of Thermodynamics is often referred to as the law of increasing entropy. Another way of looking at it is to simply understand that the default setting of *everything* is that over time, it decays and becomes more chaotic or disorganized. Different things decay at different rates—a piece of cheese left in the sun decays faster than a broken down car in a junkyard, but fundamentally everything is decaying and falling apart at some rate.

Think about your car—if you don't maintain it, it breaks down, right? Your body is the same way—if you don't take care of it, it breaks down. Guess what, your whole life is an energy system, and if you don't maintain it, it breaks down.

Now it would be easy to extrapolate what I'm saying, and come to the conclusion that we're all just doomed to fall apart. Before you do that, take a look at what I'm actually saying. I said that the *default setting* is this tendency to decay. I did not say that it's the *only possibility* for a human being. There is another option.

In 1977, Dr. Ilya Prigogine won the Nobel Prize in Chemistry for his work on what came to be known as *dissipative structures*. He noticed that even though everything in the universe has the tendency to decay, there were certain systems that displayed the opposite behavior. He noticed that certain chemical structures actually became more complex and resilient over time, and then figured out why this is. The result applies not just to chemical systems but to a human life.

From the *Journal of Applied Psychology*:

> In summary, Prigogine discovered that importation and dissipation of energy into chemical systems could reverse the maximization of entropy rule imposed by the second law of thermodynamics, that only applies to closed thermodynamic systems with no exchange of energy or entropy with the environment.

What the heck does this mean? In practical terms, it means that this increase in or maximization of entropy only applies to closed systems— systems that do not or cannot accept an influx of energy. Open systems, on the other hand, are an entirely different story. Open systems are ones that have the ability to interact with and learn from their environments, and more important, possess the ability to have energy put into them and then give energy back out.

What it means for you is very good news. As a person, you have the ability to be an open system—it's a choice that you make. The reason this is very good news is that when you exercise that choice to be an open system your life then displays the same tendency that Prigogine noticed. You buck the system; you "reverse the maximization of entropy." You literally counteract the default setting of the entire universe, and you become more adaptive and resilient over time. It's a wonderful opportunity!

The main thing you need to be cognizant of in this equation is that in an open system, energy is always flowing in and out, and here the default setting comes back into play. The outflow of energy in your life is happening without you—it just gets drained out. Because of biology, the media, our environment, other people, and a host of factors, you don't have to do anything to make energy leak out of your system. The inflow of energy will not happen unless you choose for it to happen and then act on those choices. This is the starting place of a concept that governs your life whether you realize it or not:

You are either growing or dying—there's no third option.

There's no such thing as standing still—you are either moving forward or falling behind. In an ever-expanding universe, in a world where the pace of life is accelerating at an ever-increasing rate, you cannot simply maintain. If you're not mindfully increasing the inflow of energy in your life, you are unconsciously just allowing it to drain out, unchecked.

## Your Mind Is a Flow Point

So how does this all relate to the idea and practice of aggressive mental care? Well, there are a few major flow points in your life, places where energy flows either in or out of your life, depending on how you manage them. The three big ones are:

- Your body
- Your environment
- Your mind

This makes sense if you think about it. If you're body is healthy, it gives you energy. When it's sick or injured it drains your energy. Your external environment (home, office, car, yard, family) is the same. Depending on how your environment is constructed, it will either give you energy or suck it from you. The next two chapters will address specific ways you can manage your body and your environment for stronger inflow. Your mind, however, is the central flow point of the three. Your body affects your energy through your mind. Your environment can only affect your energy through your mind. Conversely, your mind and your thoughts actually create the environment and the body that's giving or taking your energy in the first place. So by caring for your thoughts (practicing aggressive mental care), you impact positively the central flow point of energy in your life.

Think of it like a farm field. If you take a perfectly prepared, plowed and fertilized field and plant corn in it, what will grow? That's right, corn ... and weeds.

You don't need to plant the weeds; they grow all by themselves. In fact, if you don't take steps to keep the weeds out they will actually choke out the corn you want to grow. Your own corn is made up of the thoughts that uplift your life. Your weeds are the negative, self-limiting or self-destructive thoughts that pull you down. Have you noticed that negative thoughts just seem to happen all by themselves? You don't need to cultivate them, do you? To begin to understand how to grow more of a harvest, rather than just a bunch of weeds let's get a plain English understanding of how to influence your thoughts.

## What Is "Attitude"?

When people start thinking about how to influence the flow point of your mind, the word that gets used most frequently is "attitude." Attitude may be the word most frequently used by parents, coaches, and professional speakers in the last century, which is great. You hear all kinds of wonderful quotes, such as:

"Attitude is everything!"

"Attitudes are contagious—is yours worth catching?"

"It's your attitude, rather than your aptitude, which will determine your altitude."

All of these are true. Earl Nightingale said that you literally "become what you think about," one of the most powerful truths expressed in the last 100 years, but let's clearly define what we mean. When I ask participants in our workshops how they would define the word attitude, the word "outlook" is the one that comes up most often. This is close, but not complete. The definition we at Freedom Personal Development use is:

Your attitude is the way you choose to view your world.

Yes, attitude is a matter of outlook (how you view your world), but the key word in this definition is *choose*. The role of choice in your mindset is critical. In order to train our thoughts in a more positive or productive direction, the first understanding necessary is that we ultimately choose our thoughts.

Ultimately, the overall direction and quality of our thoughts is something we each choose daily, and the fact that we choose is wonderfully empowering. Why? Remember the CIA model? There are things in life we must accept, things we can Influence, and things we control. It's a lie to say that we control our thoughts directly. We do not *control* our thoughts. We have some *influence* over our thoughts, but a lot of the thoughts that arise in our minds just happen randomly. What we do have control over, however, is which thoughts we choose to focus on and what we choose to do with those thoughts.

Who does this mean is responsible for your attitude? Clearly, the responsibility is yours. If your attitude is a choice, that means that it's you and only you who's in charge of it. The quality of your thoughts is not to be delegated to your boss, your spouse, your kids, or your co-workers. It's not a result of the economy or your job, the outcome of a sporting event, or any other external circumstance. The quality of your thoughts is your responsibility—yours alone. The reason this is so empowering is that if you and you alone are responsible for your attitude, then you and you alone get to decide upon it.

You get to choose—how awesome is that?

How important is this choice?

Nobody reading a book like this would say that the thoughts and the attitude we choose are unimportant, but I'll take it a step further.

Your attitude—how you choose to view your world—is literally a matter of life and death.

When I say it's a matter of life and death, I don't mean just figuratively. I mean that at least once in everyone's life, everyone will make a choice in their mind that literally either kills them or saves their life.

My friend Mike was the clearest example I can think of. Mike worked with my company, and the first thing you'd have noticed about Mike when we worked together is that he's 6'9", about 260 pounds of lean muscle—he's a big boy. The second thing you'd notice is that he had an aura of positive energy that just surrounds him. If you've ever known anyone who makes you feel better just by being in the same room with you, Mike was definitely that guy—always smiling, always elevating other people. You could just tell that he wakes up in the morning and says, "This is going to be a great day."

Well, Mike suffered a terrible accident. Without giving all the gory details, he sustained a head injury that caused significant bruising to the frontal lobe of his brain. He got knocked into a coma-like state and the doctors had to perform a "burr hole for subdural hematoma"—also known as "they had to drill a hole in his skull to relieve the pressure." If you need this procedure, you haven't had a good day. Your life usually hangs in the balance.

Some of us who worked with Mike got to visit him a few days after he sustained the injury. He was still unconscious, and we asked his doctor for the prognosis. Please keep in mind this isn't actually me speaking here. This came from one of the most highly trained brain surgeons in the world. Pay close attention.

The doctor said, "I don't know what's going to happen with Mike, because I don't know Mike. I've seen cases much worse than Mike's where the individual returned to a perfectly normal, productive life. I've also seen cases much less severe than Mike's where the individual died very quickly. A person's chances of surviving through and then thriving after an injury like this have a lot to do with the individual. Specifically, *it has everything to do with the individual's attitude.*"

*It has everything to do with the individual's attitude.*

That's what the doctor said. Fortunately for Mike, as we mentioned, he was the king of attitude. The facts are that Mike began his recovery process shortly after that and was able to leave the hospital about 75 percent faster than even the most optimistic projections, and has done quite well since. His recovery was miraculous enough that the medical community made a study of Mike's case. The interesting thing they discovered was that, other than his height, there was nothing genetically or physiologically different about him that would indicate the remarkable speed of his recovery. The only thing they could find that separated Mike from every other case? That's right, it was his attitude. The way Mike chose to view his world literally saved his life.

When I say that your attitude is a matter of life and death, I'm not exaggerating.

## The Big Problem with Your Mind

With literally your entire life hinging on the quality of your thoughts, you must be aware of the big problem. It's found in your brain—remember the reticular activating system (RAS)? Again, that's the part of your brain that, as soon as you decide you're going to buy a red BMW makes you start noticing all the red BMWs. When that thing is tuned into success characteristics or a success vibration, it's great because it will automatically create positive thoughts and pull you toward successful situations and outcomes. So it would be great if the RAS's default setting was hardwired for success—but it's not. Your RAS—your whole brain really—is not hardwired for success. It's hardwired for survival. Your brain is fantastically efficient at keeping you alive, so over hundreds and thousands of generations it developed some wiring that worked well for survival in the wilderness, but nowadays just makes you negative and drains your energy. Somewhere along the way, your reticular activating system developed a profoundly negative tilt. It overemphasizes negative and deemphasizes positive.

This tendency used to be a tremendous asset, when survival was the whole game. Again, the RAS is essentially pattern recognition software. To have this part of your brain be hypersensitive to negative or threatening input is extremely valuable when your survival is at issue most days. The guy that either didn't notice or didn't care about the sabertooth tiger stalking him or the neighboring tribe that wanted to take over his village didn't make it very long. So back then, you really needed an early-warning mechanism that picked up on threats very early so you could avoid them or fight them. Back in that day, a hypersensitivity to negative patterns was actually more urgent to survival than the ability to recognize positive patterns like food and medicinal plants. So again, this survival mechanism in your brain is awesome if survival is the main issue.

The deal now though is that you don't really care about just survival. If you have the inclination and the time to read a book on how to *Train Your Brain for Success*, your thinking is well past survival. You want to go beyond; you want to thrive. A survival mentality won't create the breakthroughs you are looking for. A survival mentality by definition is conservative, safe, and will cause you to contract your thinking. This is the very opposite of a breakthrough or even a thriving mentality, which is growth-oriented, expansionary, and somewhat risky. What this means is that if you want your brain to get you where you want to go, you must override this survival mechanism. This is a big problem—your mind will hold onto what works for survival very tightly.

## The Good News about Your Mind

The good news is that this survival mechanism and its negative thinking definitely can be overridden—you absolutely can do it! Again, it will not happen overnight. Your brain has some habits that it is very comfortable with even if those habits don't actually work. To retrain your brain is not an easy task. It will require diligent, persistent, intelligent work on yourself, and it will require an investment on your part. It will also take some time. To permanently reset the thermostat of your mind cannot happen in less than three weeks. It takes a minimum of 21 days to form a new habit or replace an old one. But you can do it—it will just take some work.

Go back to the story of my friend Mike, the young man who bruised his brain and then recovered so well. The real lesson from Mike's story is that he didn't magically develop the attitude that saved his life while he was lying unconscious in the hospital. He developed it day by day. His mindset was, as Earl Nightingale said, a "habit-knit way of thinking and doing." How do we know this? You could tell by the way he came out of his coma. When Mike woke up he had a very specific reaction that he had trained into himself on a deep level. Anyone who knew him could have spotted it. For several years, Mike had cultivated the habit, immediately upon waking in the morning, of smiling and saying out loud,

"It's gonna be a great day."

And when he came out of his coma-like state —disoriented, in pain, and on life support—it was the most natural thing in the world for him. It was a trained-in, automatic anchor that set him on his way. He opened his eyes, looked at the hospital bed he was in, saw his family in the next room, and the very first words from his mouth were:

"It's gonna be a great day."

That doesn't happen by accident, but it does happen. And it can happen for you. Do you want the kind of resiliency that pulls you through tough times, even life and death times? Do you want the kind of energy that makes you unstoppable? Do you want a genuine internal smile that attracts the people and the situations that make your life rich? All of those are possible, and they are among the greatest gifts you can give yourself. These gifts will not be given to you by the world—it's not the world's job. But you can give them to yourself, and it only takes a little bit of retraining of your brain.

How to do it is covered in the next two chapters.

**Reinforcement and Bonuses:** This chapter has been Memory Optimized™ for your benefit. For your brief lesson and some great bonuses, visit www.planetfreedom .com/trainyourbrain with the access code on page 232. Enjoy!

# 16

# Your Energy Management Tools

W e finished the last chapter discussing the big problem about your mind (that its powerful survival mechanism will keep you stuck if left to its own tendencies), and the good news about your mind (that you fundamentally have the power and authority to override this survival mechanism). The really good news in this area is that you also have built into you five terrific tools for accomplishing this override. Let me stress that everyone has these tools, including you. You always have access to them, and for the most part they don't cost a penny. You can use any or all of them at any time, and the more you use them the better you will get with them. I'll help you understand what they are and how they can help you train your brain.

## Tool #1: Your Ability to Laugh...

Your first energy management tool is your ability to laugh. Have you ever noticed how a good laugh just makes you feel better?

There's a reason for it—laughter actually affects your brain in much the same way as good drugs. Now I'm not advocating recreational drug use, but I am advocating recreational laughter use as a way of managing and amplifying your energy levels. A good laugh does so many good things for your body and brain, and the results are well documented. Here is a quote from *Science Daily* (April 2010):

> Norman Cousins first suggested the idea that humor and the associated laughter can benefit a person's health in the 1970s. His ground-breaking work, as a layperson diagnosed with an autoimmune disease, documented his use of laughter in treating himself—with medical approval and oversight—into remission. He published his personal research results in the *New England Journal of Medicine* and is considered one of the original architects of mind-body medicine.

Since then the number of medical conditions that have been found to positively respond to regular laughter has absolutely skyrocketed. From diabetes and obesity to any number of cardiovascular problems to (in some cases) even cancer have all been documented to be positively impacted by regular laughter as part of the treatment. Day to day, some of the benefits of laughter are:

- It burns calories.
- It stretches your muscles.
- It feels great.
- It releases a number of terrifically healthy hormones— endorphins, dopamine, serotonin, and HGH, to name a few.
- It makes you more attractive.
- It reduces or alleviates negative stress.

A good laugh is among the best energy boosters we have available to us, and the great news about this is that we all have the ability to laugh! I spent eight years doing professional stand-up comedy, but I want to stress that you do not need to be a comedian to access and use this tool. It's not necessarily your ability to make other people laugh, it's your own ability to laugh, in three specific ways:

## ... At Yourself

Start with your ability to laugh *at yourself*. I've often thought that one of the major causes of the negative stress we experience is that we just take ourselves too seriously! We think that whatever problem we're experiencing right now will:

a. Ruin us forever.
b. Never be understood by anyone else.
c. Never end.

And most of the time, you know that it just ain't true! I've found that we always have the choice, in any given situation, to decide how seriously we'll take ourselves. The ability to laugh at ourselves is never about *can versus can't*. It's always about *will versus won't*. If you're somebody who won't laugh at yourself, I'm just obligated to make you aware of two things. First: If you won't laugh at yourself, *other people will feel the need to do it for you*. Second: It's my observation that those who don't laugh at themselves find themselves in situations where they look more ridiculous than average, more often than average, until they learn to lighten up.

I'm not saying that you shouldn't take your life and your work seriously, and I'm certainly not saying that you shouldn't take the needs of your family or your clients seriously. I'm just saying don't take *yourself* too seriously. Placing yourself at the center of the universe requires an enormous amount of energy. That's energy which can serve you much better if directed elsewhere.

## ...With Other People

Next, learn to laugh *with other people*. Not at other people, *with* other people. All of us are involved in building relationships with other people—we need help to make our lives move forward. And the ability to laugh with other people is one of the fastest ways to break down barriers that keep us apart.

In my sales career, I got some great advice early on. I actually got the same advice twice in a three-week span from two very different sources. In a sales seminar, an instructor said that, "If you can laugh with your customers, they will buy from you. End of story." I thought this was sound advice. Slightly oversimplified, but sound nonetheless, so I took it to heart. I may have actually taken it too much to heart, because three weeks later, one of my customers gave me the same advice, but in a very different way.

I was selling educational books door-to-door in western Pennsylvania. After making a sale to a family, the father took me aside and said "Roger, I've been involved in sales and sales management for 25 years, and there's something that as a salesperson, you do better than I've ever seen." Feeling very cool, I said "Really! Well, what is it?" He looked me dead in the eye and said:

"Roger, I've found that it's nearly impossible to say no to a smiling idiot."

Looking back, I'm pretty sure this was meant as a compliment. And it's been very helpful advice in my sales career.

## ...About Negative Situations

Listen, we all have problems. You can call them challenges, situations, and opportunities if you like (terrific idea—more on your language in a bit), but fundamentally we all have negative situations to deal with. People who don't like us, obstacles to our achieving our goals, terrible market conditions, competition we didn't ask for, and the list goes on and on. The faster we learn to laugh about our negative situations, the faster we elevate our thinking and develop the key to solving our problems and perspective. Einstein said that, "We cannot solve problems on the same level of thinking that created them in the first place."

Have you ever had a seemingly enormous problem that you looked back on and laughed? It's extremely common, so why not try laughing about it while it's happening? Again, I'm not trying to belittle your problems—just try it out. The next time you've got something bad happening, *why not* look for the humor in it? I can't tell you how many times just looking for something funny in a bad business deal or a tough audience or a big mistake was *the* thing that helped me reframe what was going on in a way that sparked the solution in my mind.

Here is a tip for cultivating your ability to laugh:

Learn to think like a four-year-old—preschoolers are the happiest thinkers. They:

a. Say what's on their mind, immediately.
b. Never carry a grudge for more than about five minutes.
c. Are always looking on the bright side.
d. Think creatively.
e. Are endlessly amused by the simplest things.

We can do all of these things if only we choose them.

## Tool #2: Your Ability to Practice Gratitude

Perhaps the fastest energy booster is the emotion of gratitude. My business partner Eric Plantenberg said it best:

*"It's impossible to be grateful and negative at the same time."*

This quote has been so useful to me. If I'm feeling low, I have found that the simple act of taking one moment to focus on what I am genuinely thankful for produces an instantaneous boost of energy. I've also found that focusing on what makes me grateful for a few minutes causes that boost to last for several hours. If you're looking to boost your mood quickly, the antidote to negativity is gratitude. Do yourself a favor right now—answer this question:

*Do you have at least one thing in your life that you are genuinely thankful for?*

Of course—I've never met anyone who doesn't have at least one. Take a moment and focus on whatever it was that just popped into your mind. See it as clearly as you can. How do you feel right now? Better, yes? The emotion of gratitude, even in very small amounts, causes a pretty specific neurological/biochemical chain reaction that does great things for your energy. Best part: It does these things instantaneously.

Now let's take it one step further. Practicing gratitude on a regular, systematic basis actually trains your brain to seek out and attract positive inputs, *which positively alters your whole world.* In every moment we have a choice of where to place our attention. Think back to the introduction to this book—remember the principle of what you see is what you get? Remember how the pictures that we see in our minds tend to be the results we get? Watch this. You just identified at least one thing that you're thankful for. A little while ago we discussed how we all have problems as well. So if the principle of what you see is what you get is true at all, when you focus on your problems what will your mind attract more of? You got it, problems. If you will train yourself to focus regularly on the things you are thankful for, your mind will see them more often, and when you do that, guess what? Right again—you actually attract more things that you will be thankful for. Your focus determines and creates your reality.

Practicing gratitude utilizes what's known in quantum physics as the *observer effect*. The *observer effect* essentially means that in a given experiment, a particle will be in a particular place based on whether or not the experimenter *expects* it to be there.

Literally, experimenters affect the outcome of experiments by what they think. In our lives, thoughts of gratitude versus resentment operate much the same way. Have you ever noticed that people who complain a lot usually have a lot to complain about, that bad news begets more bad news? And have you ever noticed that the opposite is true—that good news begets more good news?

Even better, have you ever looked back on a seemingly terrible situation and realized it was actually one of the best things that ever happened to you? My dad was a great example of this. My dad would have been the first to tell you that his spiritual life was nonexistent to weak for most of his life. Earlier I mentioned my family history with colon cancer. In 1999 my dad was diagnosed with colon cancer, and it was far enough along that it was obvious he was going to die from it. The treatment was as bad as the disease in many ways, and over the next few years his body began to just break down. It would have been extremely easy for him to be resentful, but he went the other way. Being deathly ill and scared about it actually caused him to enjoy his life more than he ever thought possible. Shortly before he passed away, I asked him how he was doing with the whole experience.

He said (I'm paraphrasing here) "My body kind of sucks, but I am really grateful for what's happening."

I was really surprised to hear this, and I said, "Wow, how is that?"

He replied (and now I'm not paraphrasing) "Well, knowing my life will be over soon has done something I didn't expect. You know that I never really could see God in my everyday life. *Now I see God everywhere.*"

Whoa.

Practicing gratitude—the act of focusing on what you are thankful for—is the single fastest way I know of for changing your physiology, shaping your life positively, and boosting your energy level.

Tips for cultivating an attitude of gratitude:

1. Keep a gratitude journal. We've discussed in a few places how writing things down makes them more real for your mind. Having a gratitude journal where you literally take notes on the things that you are thankful for is an extremely powerful way of training your brain to focus on and attract grateful thoughts and the accompanying results. If you can't or don't want to have an actual journal, you can just set an alarm for yourself every day that triggers you to take a few minutes to focus on anything you're grateful for, large or small. Sounds cheesy, but it works like a miracle for creating an instant energy boost.

2. Do things that you would be grateful for. This is an area where you will very much get back what you put out. When you create gratitude in your world, you will get more of it. A Buddhist might say: "It is impossible to light the path of another without also lighting your own." Think about the last time you did something nice for someone, even as small as opening a door or returning something you saw them drop. They were obviously thankful for getting the small gift, and then *you felt great for giving it!* You got the double bonus!

## Tool #3: Your Ability to Manage Mental Input Sources

You've heard the brain described as the world's most powerful computer, and in many ways that's true. There's a phrase from the world of computer programming that definitely applies to your brain:

Garbage In = Garbage Out.

A computer can't make judgments about the programming it receives. It just executes the program *exactly as it has been instructed*. Your subconscious mind is the same. It doesn't question its programming, it just executes powerfully. So if you want to see record-breaking results, you'd better be running a record-breaking program in your mind. Your mind's programming comes from its input sources, of which there are five:

1. What you read
2. What you watch
3. What you listen to
4. The people you surround yourself with
5. Your language

Critical concept: Keep in mind your RAS's default setting. When it comes to your mental input sources, if you are not consciously making them positive and energy-boosting, you are unconsciously allowing them to be negative and energy draining. There is no third option, there is no middle ground. Positive input sources are never, ever an accident.

The following are some examples of being conscious versus unconscious with your input sources.

## What You Read

Whether you realize it or not, you are reading things all the time, either consciously or unconsciously. You can consciously read a book, magazine, or newspaper as you're doing right now, which simply means you've made a choice to pick some reading material up and allow it into your brain. Ideally, you're asking the three Smart Reading questions: "Why am I reading this?" "What do I need this information for/what am I looking for?" and "How much time do I have?". This will always produce a positive result, even if you are just reading for entertainment. The reason is that if nothing else, you strengthen your choosing muscles. If what you're reading is information that impacts your life positively, so much the better.

Unconscious reading usually looks like walking by something (a newspaper, a magazine at the grocery store, a billboard) and reading it in passing. What gets into your brain when you do that? Headlines and advertisements—is either of these really good for you?

## What You Watch

According to Nielsen, the average American watches TV 142 hours per month. That's over 4.5 hours per day, every day. This may be the single biggest energy drain that we as a country experience. 4.5 hours a day? Are you kidding me? If that's you—stop it. Let me be very clear on this issue:

*If you watch four hours of TV every day, you will not achieve your goals. Period.*

Talk to anyone who leads their field, and ask them about TV watching. Many you will find actually do watch television, but very little, and *always with a purpose*. Many will watch shows that relate to their field, or to keep up on current events, or they will have one show that they watch for entertainment. However they watch, they do it consciously. None of them spends four hours a day vegging in front of a screen—none. It's not actually about the number of hours, it's just that the very act of zoning out in front of the flat screen is an act of unconsciousness. It's impossible to be devoting almost 20 percent of your life to that act and not have massive hemorrhaging of your energy supply.

As we said about your brain, it is biologically attracted to motion. Throw in the knowledge that we think in pictures, and then throw in the idea that the more clear and vivid and emotionalized our mental pictures are the more they stick in your mind. Do you understand now why the messages that come through the TV are so influential? Do you get why corporations spend way over 50 billion dollars annually on TV advertising? Bottom line is that TV affects your brain like a drug, and what you see there will stick. Have you ever noticed how watching a scary movie right before bed will disrupt your sleep? Have you ever fallen asleep in front of the TV and actually dreamed that you were in an infomercial? If it's on, the TV is an extremely powerful influence.

So contrary to where you may think I'm going here, I am not going to tell you to blow up your television, although I know a lot of successful people who will just eliminate TV when they have a major goal. What you really need to do is make a conscious choice about what you watch. There are lots of great things about TV, movies, and Internet videos, as long as you are mindful about what you allow into your mind. I just don't believe you can do that 4.5 hours a day.

## What You Listen to

Almost as impactful as what you watch is what you listen to—music, talk radio, sports—are you making a conscious choice about this input source? Again, you can either consciously make this input source energy boosting or unconsciously allow it to be energy draining.

There's a huge opportunity here because:

1. You can actually use this input source while doing other things.
2. The sheer amount of knowledge you can gain while exercising, driving, grocery shopping, showering, doing housework, and other otherwise mundane activities is staggering.

The practice of listening to educational audios and consciously chosen inspirational music for at least some of the time in your car and during other activities is one of the absolute most profitable choices you can make. In August 2011, my friend Tom Weber and I both committed that for one month we would not listen to the radio while driving—only audio that we had chosen. Both of us were spending several hours daily in the car, so this was not the easiest challenge. What happened was astounding. Tom immediately had by far the highest sales productivity our company had ever seen and has maintained that new level. For me, the results were slightly delayed, but in October and November of that year I shattered our company's longstanding monthly and quarterly sales record. Worth it?

So shut off the radio for a little while, and make a more positive choice. For a list of our all-time favorite listening material, check the "Reinforcement and Bonus" section at the end of this chapter.

## The People You Surround Yourself with

Maybe your most profound input source is the people you spend your time with. In my speeches, I'll usually find someone who has teenage kids and ask them:

"If your teenager were going out, what would be the first two questions you'd ask?"

Without fail, if it isn't the first question it's the second: "Who are you going with?" Parents want to know this, because they instinctively know that *their kid will become like the kids they hang out with*, at least for a while. They also know that if they hang out with a certain crowd long enough, they become like that permanently. Finally, they know that this influence can either work for a kid or against them, but it is always working.

Guess what—that peer group influence is happening to you right now. You are becoming like the kids you hang out with. If they are bringing you up, wonderful! If not, perhaps a change is in order. Brian Tracy says that "the selection of a negative peer group, all by itself can completely ruin a career." Want a good indicator of your income five years from now? Look at the income of your five best friends currently. Don't misunderstand—I'm not saying you should ditch all your poor friends. I'm saying that you must be conscious of the influence your friends have on your life, and make adjustments if necessary. You can't change the result of a negative input source; you can only change the source itself.

## Your Language

The last mental input source we'll discuss here is your language—how you speak. There are a couple of aspects to your language.

One is your *self-talk*. Are you aware that your mind is always talking to you? Twenty-four hours a day, you are always talking to yourself. If you monitor that conversation, you'll notice that unless you are being mindful of it, that conversation will have a profoundly negative, doubtful, fearful tone. I sound like a broken record, but if you don't consciously make your self-talk positive and energy-boosting, it will be negative and energy-draining.

The second is the *questions you ask, specifically when dealing with problems*. I have found that in life there are winners and losers. When confronted with *adversity*, losers will tend think in generalities, and they tend to ask *why*.

"Why did this happen to me?"

"Why are people so mean?"

"Why don't I ever get the breaks?"

Winners on the other hand will tend to think in specifics, and they tend to ask *how*. As in "how can I fix this?"

"How can I avoid this in the future?"

"How can I learn from this experience?"

Different questions will bring different answers. You must avoid the mind's tendency to be generally negative. Instead, cultivate the habit of being specifically positive.

Here are some tips for more effectively managing your input sources:

1. Cultivate the habit of reading a book on personal development for 30 minutes a day. 60 is better, 15 is mandatory for breaking records.
2. Shut off your TV for a week, and watch the miracles that happen.
3. Take the challenge to listen to personal development audios in your car instead of the radio for a month. At least try it for a week.

4. Take inventory of the influence your personal associations are having. Do you need more of some people? Less of others? Notice this and act accordingly.

5. Read the book *What to Say When You Talk to Yourself*, by Dr. Shad Helmstetter. It's where I personally learned the science and the practice of verbal affirmations. The year I read it, I tripled my income and had way more fun.

## Tool #4: Your Ability to Decide Your Focus

Your focus literally creates your reality. We've already discussed this in a bunch of ways in this book; I've quoted Covey, "All things are created twice." We've talked a little bit about the power of visualization and the law of attraction. A few pages ago, you learned about the observer effect—how even on a quantum level, the focus we have actually creates experiment results.

And I'm certainly not the first one to make this assertion. From Napoleon Hill to Earl Nightingale to Thomas Edison to Albert Einstein to the father of modern-day American psychology, William James, all the great minds have understood and asserted that what we focus our mind on literally gets created. Same thing with our energy, and the focus or creation link is often instantaneous. When you shift your focus from "what's wrong" to "what's right," you change your energy and vibration immediately.

Fortunately for us humans, our focus is under our control. The single biggest thing that makes us human is the ability to choose what we pay attention to. Animals do not have this ability. Yes, our minds have some pretty destructive tendencies. If left untended in this society, your mind will likely lead you places you really don't want to be and it will keep you stuck there. But we are not slaves to our tendencies—we can decide differently. And we can do it on a moment-by-moment basis.

Tips for strengthening this tool:

1. Go back to the entire section on energizing goals and really do those exercises. Fundamentally, there's no better or more powerful way to enhance your focus and train your brain to keep its attention on your goals.
2. Really do the Two-Hour Solution. I know these aren't fancy tips, but this is where the rubber meets the road.

## Tool #5: Your Ability to Take Action

Ultimately it's *action* that directly creates your results. If you always do what you've always done, you'll always get what you've always gotten.

One of the thinking models we teach in our workshops is called Be, Do, Have. This is how your life essentially unfolds. Your character and your thinking (the Be), creates and guides your actions (the Do), which then creates your results (the Have). There are many wonderful understandings and quotes that stem from this model—it could probably be the subject of an entire book itself. *Train Your Brain* is all about how to make your life better soon, so for now, understand that:

While the Be influences the Do, the Do also influences the Be.

Your thinking impacts your actions, and your actions also impact your thoughts. Ever noticed how getting up and walking around boosts your energy? Ever noticed how when you smile at someone, *you* feel better? Or how cleaning out your car actually makes you more energetic? It's often easier to impact your energy by starting with the Do-ing. *It's usually easier to act your way to healthy thinking than it is to think your way to healthy acting.*

So get into action!

Here are some specific action steps proven to boost energy:

1. Smile, even if you don't feel like it. It does several things to your brain that boost performance and mood.

2. Take any form of physical exercise. The connection between a healthy body and a healthy mind couldn't be clearer. Even just a 15-minute walk or a dozen push-ups can really clear your mind and provide a great energy boost.

3. Do something nice for someone else. We covered this under practicing gratitude.

4. Take charge of your environment. Clean the garage, straighten your room, get a haircut, get the car washed, anything to improve the state of your environment.

Tim Ferriss, author of the monster bestseller *The 4-Hour Body*, put it this way. When he was asked about how a person could "improve their inner game" his instant reply was "improve your outer game." It's true that real, lasting change comes from the inside out. Often, however, we can impact the inside through improving the outside. Do, Be, Do, Have.

Chapter 17 will teach you how to create your own Power Hour, a specific daily energy management practice that allows you to implement all of these tools. You'll learn how to create an undefeated mentality in a way that's simple, extremely productive, and fun.

**Reinforcement and Bonuses:** This chapter has been Memory Optimized™ for your benefit. For your brief lesson and some great bonuses, visit www.planetfreedom .com/trainyourbrain with the access code on page 232. Enjoy!

# 17

# The Power Hour: Your Daily Energy Management Practice

Before we get into this chapter, I want to congratulate you on getting this far in *Train Your Brain For Success*. Statistics show that something like 90 percent of personal development books that get bought do not get finished, and you're almost there! I know there's a feeling of relief and accomplishment when you finish something important. You feel like you've gained a victory!

That's what this final chapter is all about—how to predictably create that feeling of victory every day. When you develop a habitual pattern of victory, you go a long way toward being completely unstoppable.

## The Value of the "Last 5 Percent"

I was talking with somebody recently about where he was getting stuck in his business. He said, "I know that I need to do 100

**217**

percent of what needs to be done, including the little things. I'm at about 95 percent, but I'm seeing that 100 percent is necessary." We then talked about a principle of physical training that applies to a person's productivity.

In any workout—for improved endurance or strength—the actual growth stimulus occurs in a very small portion of the work- out: *the last 1 to 5 percent* of the entire workout. For instance, if you're doing 3 sets of 10 reps on the bench press, you will only see enhanced muscle performance if the weight you use causes the last couple of reps of the last set to be nearly impossible. If those last few reps are easy, you have not taxed the muscle enough, and you will see exactly zero improvement. If a five-mile training run is to boost your endurance or speed, it should be run so that the last half mile is nearly impossible. If you're not "out of gas" at the end, your run was too easy and you won't get faster. This is not my opinion; this is exercise science. There are many theories as to the best way to get physical results, all of them revolve around the concept of pushing your workout to the "point of failure."

Two important principles are:

1. The whole workout must be done, but the first 95 percent of the workout is done for the sole purpose of taxing your body to the point where it can receive a growth stimulus. That first 95 percent is necessary, but it doesn't actually produce a result.
2. The last 5 percent is where the results happen. As you approach, then cross the threshold of giving out, this is the only part of the workout that actually makes your body do what it does to make you stronger, faster, or better. This also happens to be the part of the workout that hurts the most.

So in effect this individual was doing the first 95 percent of the workout, but not the last 5 percent. Now you'd think that if you do 95 percent of the workout that you'd get 95 percent of the results, but that is clearly not the case. In an actual workout, if you're doing 95 percent, you get *zero results*. You make no improvement—ever. This is why you see people who go to the gym year after year in an effort to get fitter, but they just maintain.

In life and in business the same concept applies. If you're only 95 percent, you miss out on all of what produces results. Some examples are:

— If you dial a phone number 95 percent correctly, you don't get someone who knows the person you're trying to reach. You get a wrong number.

— If you get 95 percent of the way to a restaurant, do you get 95 percent of your dinner?

— In sales, if you get 95 percent of the way through your sales presentation, but fail to ask for the business, you don't get 95 percent of the business. You get nothing.

— How many times have we seen a day of appointment setting stats like "100 dials and 3 appointments set," where the bookings happened on dials 95, 97, and 100? Answer—a ton.

— How many months have we seen where a company went from disappointing sales results to exciting sales results in the last few days of the month? Answer—a ton.

So what's *your* last 5 percent? What are the little things in your life or business that get you all the results? For me it's things like confirming appointments three to five days in advance, not one or two. Like listening to audio programs instead of the radio. Like getting to bed at 9 or 9:30, not 10. There could be a whole host of last 5 percent things. Make sure that you are seeing projects 100 percent of the way through, not just 95 percent. The last 5 percent is where you actually get the results you're looking for.

The last 5 percent of *Train Your Brain for Success* is about that last 5 percent in your life. We're going to take everything you've learned in the previous 16 chapters and tie it all together into a daily practice that will:

- Skyrocket your energy levels.
- Keep you on track.
- Tune your brain to a positive results frequency every day.
- Anchor you to your values, your goals, your purpose.
- Fire up your attitude of gratitude.
- Make you physically healthier.
- Create a perfect space in your day for any other personal development you wish to do.
- Cause members of the opposite sex to think you're extremely hot.

Well, maybe not the last one—but it won't hurt.

This practice (which we call the *Power Hour*) is the practice that I've personally crafted for myself over the last several years to consistently break records in every area of my life. My company and I have taught it to clients around the world and we know it works. I'll teach you specifically what I do, but more importantly I'll teach you the principles behind it so you can craft your own. I'll also give you modifications I've seen people make that have worked.

## Where This Comes from—The Concept of "Little Victories"

In my early 20s I worked with The Southwestern Company, selling educational books door-to-door. I made great money and had a lot of fun, but the best thing was the life lessons that I learned. One of the best was taught to me by a top salesperson, a young man who made the equivalent of a six-figure income as a college student. In talking about how he got such incredible results, he described what he called "little victories"—a series of a few things he did to start each day that got him mentally prepped for a great day. I started doing them and saw great results myself. Through that I learned that small wins in controllable areas create momentum that carries into every area.

A few years later I read *The 7 Habits of Highly Effective People* and read about the concept of how "*private victories precede public victories.*" It clicked for me how the victories we achieve when nobody is watching are the foundation for the wins we experience when everyone is watching. John Wooden said that "Champions are made when nobody's looking."

So I realized that my "little victories" list that worked so well in a very specific sales environment was actually a microcosm of how to effectively build real momentum systematically in a person's life, and that anyone could do it. Thus began the development of the Power Hour.

## What the Power Hour Does

Scientifically, a morning routine like the Power Hour will establish neural pathways that activate several systems in your brain to:

1. Elevate your vibrational frequency.
2. Release positive, life-enhancing hormones and neurochemicals.
3. Impact your environment on a quantum level to attract and create the exact circumstances, people, and ideas you need to create your ideal life.

If none of that made sense or you don't care about the science, here's a more practical analogy. If you were a pro athlete, you wouldn't even consider taking the field or the court for a game without a warm-up period, for both the body and the mind. In fact, you wouldn't do that if you were playing a game of pick-up basketball or going golfing. So why on earth would you ever consider starting a day—the fundamental unit of time where you play the game of your life—without warming up?

The Power Hour gets both your mind and your body ready for a great day, and it unquestionably improves both energy levels and performance.

## The Power Hour Described

The Power Hour has evolved into a specific series of small actions that I take on a daily basis. I'll lay out what I'm doing right now, which is in the first quarter of 2011. Feel free to adopt this routine wholesale, feel free to pick and choose parts, feel free to add to it, and definitely feel free to change it up. My friend Alan Mong (who's taken this concept to a whole new level for himself and for me), actually advocates purposely switching it up every few months to keep it fresh. Great idea.

To start with, however, one of the most important concepts is that in order to get the maximum benefit from this protocol, you'll need to do the same routine consistently for a minimum of three weeks, and 30 days is better. Yes, you'll get a boost and a better day right away, but where the Power Hour really starts to affect deep and significant changes is when it becomes a *habit*. To cement a *habit* actually requires the creation of and the setting of a new neural pathway in your brain, which requires a minimum of 21 days of repetition. So take this template and use it to create something that you will commit to doing for a month. If it's only a Power Half-hour that's fine. Craft it to fit you and then get going on it immediately. You will notice a difference.

Currently, I've got 15 things that I do every day as my Power Hour. Each of the 15 things is an action that I do mindfully and purposefully—there's a specific reason for it. Each action either

— anchors me to what's important to me.
— does something specific to tune my brain to a success frequency.
— is something I kind of don't like (it's a small victory over my lower self), or:
— is just a healthy habit.

You could say that each day starts the night before. There are three things that I do before bed to set up a great start to the next day. These were mentioned in a couple of places earlier, but just to review:

- I take a moment to review the day, practice gratitude, and just let the day go. Positive or negative, the events of the day are now in the past and cannot be repeated unless I choose to repeat them.
- I do my Daily Big Six for the next day. Again, deciding upon your most important results the night before allows your subconscious mind to work on them while you're asleep.
- I set an alarm for when I want to get up the next morning. While my brain is winding down from waking to sleeping, I gently say to myself "tomorrow's gonna be a great day!"

Now I'm preloaded for a great Power Hour the next morning. Here's how the first hour of the day goes for me, along with why each step is effective:

1. My alarm goes off and I physically get out of bed—I do not hit the snooze alarm. The reason this is important for me is twofold:
   a. I decided last night what time I was getting up, and it builds strength and self-esteem when you make and then honor a commitment to yourself (even a small one like not hitting the snooze alarm).
   b. For me (like most) the comfort of my nice warm bed has a fairly strong pull, and I find it encouraging that within the very first few seconds of the day I've made a decision that favors enthusiasm and energy over mere comfort.

   Do you recall our discussion of the comfort zone? Its pull is strong, and I understand that zero growth happens in the comfort zone. My business partner Eric Plantenberg taught me to *get comfortable being uncomfortable*, and I've found that concept to be the foundational key to personal development. This may seem infinitesimally small, but this little victory is a daily reminder of this concept.

2. Immediately upon waking, I start the day with a verbal affirmation—specifically, I say out loud, "It's gonna be a great day!" In Chapter 16 we discussed the vital role of your self-talk as a mental input source. I want to take control of my language as early in the day as possible. Our thoughts influence our words—more importantly, our words influence our thoughts. Note: When I say "out loud" I don't necessarily mean "very loud"—no need to wake the neighbors. Just loud enough so that I can hear myself.

   Does this one sound a little corny? For me the whole concept of positive verbal affirmations seemed *really* hokey at first. After reading *What to Say When You Talk to Yourself*, however, I understood that affirmations truly have an incredibly powerful impact on your mind, especially in these first few moments of the morning. This practice really works. I had one client who took just this specific step and implemented it at the beginning of a new year. Three months later she informed me that, because of the chain reaction this one phrase set off in her life, she was on track to triple her income. Do not underestimate the power of this simple step.

3. I take a moment to practice gratitude. I really am grateful for my house, my health, my bed, my family, my business, and a host of other things. So as I'm moving from bedroom to bathroom (yes, that also happens for me in the morning, but it's not actually part of the Power Hour, so no need to discuss) I just reflect and see these things in my mind. Based on the law of attraction, I know that by being mindful of the things in life that bring me joy, I activate the process of pulling more of those things into my life.

4. I floss and brush my teeth—this one is just a healthy habit, plus flossing is another thing I'm just not particularly fond of. Mastery over self in small ways.

5. I go down to my kitchen and drink a full 16-oz. glass of water. Proper hydration is really important for your energy, and we usually wake up somewhat dehydrated after not drinking anything all night. A big drink of water first thing gets all the important internal systems moving in a host of different ways.

6. I start a pot of coffee, and I really enjoy the process. Yes, I literally "wake up and smell the coffee." Partly this step is counted because I really like coffee, partly it's so I don't have to buy coffee later. It anchors me to David Bach's automatic millionaire concept of the "latte factor." If you don't know what that is, read any of his books.

7. I move to my living room and set up in my "morning spot." I stand tall and take five deep breaths, all the way down into my abdomen. I visualize myself inhaling gratitude and exhaling tension. We discussed earlier how even a few deep breaths flood your brain with oxygen and calms the parasympathetic nervous system. I do this as mindfully as possible.

8. I stretch my legs and back for a few minutes. For me, mental and physical flexibility are vital concepts, so stretching impacts both. In fact, you may notice that the next few steps are actually physical reminders of philosophies and important concepts in my life

9. I do 20 to 25 deep knee bends. The specific number will depend on either a business goal or an income goal that I have that can be made to fall within this range. Again, it's a physical reminder of a psychological concept. The reason for this range is that somewhere around 20 is where I start to "feel the burn" in my leg muscles. I'm not trying to blast my legs here, just get the big muscles working.

10. I do 40 push-ups—same concept as #9, just with push-ups.

11. I do 40 sit-ups—same concept as #9 and #10, just with sit-ups.

12. Now that my brain and body are turned on (light to moderate calisthenics like these boost my heart rate somewhat, which physiologically gets energy flowing faster), I am definitely awake. If I sit back down to be still, I will not fall back asleep. So this is the point where I will read my own description of my core values, purpose, and keystone goal. These have been handwritten on 3x5 cards. Included in that stack of cards is a series of written affirmations that I've created for myself. For a good starter list of affirmations, see the "Reinforcement and Bonus" section at the end of this chapter.

13. I take anywhere between 20 and (ideally) 60 minutes to meditate. Personally, I have found tremendous benefit from a program called the Holosync Solution from Centerpointe Research Institute. It's audio technology for "entraining" brainwaves during meditation into deeper states of awareness. The science of it is a little outside the scope of this chapter, but I have found the practice of meditation to be incredibly productive in my business and in my life, and the Holosync program has taken it to a whole new level. The deal with meditation in general is that (among other things) it strengthens both your mind and your brain. If your mind creates your reality, it just follows that a stronger mind creates a stronger reality.

14. Now that my mind/brain is actually thinking more deeply, I briefly repeat step #12—I review values, purpose, goals, and affirmations.

15. Now that my mind and body are fully tuned up, I review my Daily Big 6 and make any adjustments I want.

Lastly, I mentally review everything that I just did, and I tally the score. I literally identify each specific action as a little victory and give myself a mental pat on the back.

Now I'm ready to get going with the day.

I love the last step, it's really the kicker. Remember when I talked about having an undefeated mentality? When I've done this, it's not just BS to artificially pump myself up. I've literally tallied 15 victories in my life before most of the world has even gotten out of bed! When you do this, you literally end up saying to yourself and believing, "Holy cow, I am awesome! I am 15 and 0 and I haven't even started yet! You cannot stop me, you can only hope to contain me!" You will feel fantastic, and you know what?

You will have earned it.

## Making Your Power Hour User Friendly

Does this seem a little complicated or time consuming? I can see where it might appear that way, It's certainly different from how the majority of the population wakes up. So let's be clear—how much time does this actually take? Not nearly as much as you might think. If you take out #13 (the meditation step, which ideally lasts 45 to 60 minutes for me but often is shortened because I have two young children that jump in my lap at 6:30 AM), the entire rigamarole takes about 20 minutes. This means that if I'm doing all 15 steps it's about an hour. Now really look at what that means for my psyche and self-esteem. In the very first hour of the day I've done more than a dozen things that I absolutely know have a powerful impact on my two most valuable assets: my health and my state of mind. Do you think it's worth it? It's my experience that this Power Hour is the most valuable hour of my day. When I started doing this systematically (about three years ago at the time of this writing), my business turned around, my financial situation improved dramatically, my relationships with my wife and kids also improved, and I found that I had much more energy and vitality. So even in its full, somewhat lunatic glory it's an investment that pays off hugely.

That said, feel free to make your own modifications. If your Power Hour needs to be a Power Half-hour, no problem. As I said, the important thing to take away here is to craft your own success routine, and feel free to call it what you want. The reason the Power Hour described above works well for me is that it's mine. I learned the principles from a couple of books I read and then made the principles my own. Feel free to omit some of the steps. If you only have 5 or 6 that really work for you, so be it. There are tons of other specific steps I've seen people use. Some of them include:

- Music
- Comedy
- Yoga
- Inspirational videos
- Inspirational reading
- Scripture reading
- Prayer
- Running
- Kissing and hugging family members
- Eating specific foods
- Dancing

So make it work for you! You'll find that a daily energy management practice that you like and make a habit of might do more for your life than any other single concept in this book.

**Reinforcement and Bonuses:** This chapter has been Memory Optimized™ for your benefit. For your brief lesson and some great bonuses, visit www.planetfreedom .com/trainyourbrain with the access code on page 232. Enjoy!

# Conclusion
# What to Do with What You've Learned

Congratulations—you've reached the end of *Train Your Brain For Success!* We've covered an enormous amount of information—you've gotten a big pile of ideas, strategies, and specific techniques for remembering more, reading smarter, and breaking records in any area of your life. I trust that along the way you've found and begun to unlock and unleash more of you on the world.

You've heard me say (and imply) numerous times throughout this work that it's great to get new ideas, but what's more important is what you do with those ideas. It's been said that *unused potential is humanity's greatest burden.*

So where do you go from here? In the introduction I encouraged you to take an active approach to this book and implement the strategies you find. Specifically, here are some Do's and Don'ts to help you continue your record-breaking march to victory.

1. *Do* use this book as an ongoing resource. Mark it up, highlight it, make notes in it, and come back to it often. *Don't* just let it sit on your bookshelf. This work is essentially a manual for breaking records, so refer to it often

2. *Don't* try to do everything different all at once. Pick a handful of these strategies and get to work on making them

habits. That takes 21 to 30 days, so give yourself a little time to let your new habits develop.

3. If nothing else, *do* commit to implementing the Two-Hour Solution and creating a Power Hour (or at least a Power Half-hour) for yourself. These two practices give you the necessary space to get at the root of what works for you and I've found they have the most profound impact in the shortest amount of time.

4. If you haven't done this by now (shame on you) *do* visit www.planetfreedom.com with the access code on page 232 for your Memory Optimization™ and bonus materials. Planet Freedom is a really neat community—be part of it!

And lastly, *do* feel free to reach out to me and my staff. Continue to invest time and resources in yourself. For me, I find that the books I've read have had an enormous impact on me in and of themselves. I've also found that spending time with like-minded people and/or having someone hold my hand and walk me through the process of personal development is often the next thing you need to catapult what you get from a book to the next level. If you were blown away with how much your memory or your reading skills improved here, continue the journey with a live or online workshop. If the Two-Hour Solution or the Power Hour or any other systems you developed here are already elevating your results and you want more . . . believe me, there's more. More that you can Be, more that you can Do, and for sure more that you can Have. My company and I exist to serve by delivering freedom—come and get some! We are here for you.

The impact of investing in yourself is impossible to over-state. My associates and I truly appreciate the investment you've made in yourself. Keep making it and you'll find that it's the best investment you can make.

Be free!

*Roger Seip*

# About the Author

**Roger Seip**
International Speaker and Performance Coach
Co-Founder, Freedom Personal Development

*Intelligent, insightful … and hilarious!*

These are the words that Roger's clients use when they experience his programs. He has a knack for taking principles of effectiveness that most humans struggle with and crystallizing them into clear strategies and action plans that get record-breaking results. He's also one of the world's foremost authorities on how to train the incredible creative capacity of the human mind.

When it comes to creating record-breaking results, Roger walks the walk. Some examples:

- In his first sales career, Roger became one of the top 20 producers out of over 200,000 in the 160-year history of the company. That's the top 1 percent of the top 1 percent *ever*.
- Roger co-founded Freedom Personal Development, one of the world's premier personal development firms. His company has thrived and broken records for more than 15 years.
- Roger has personally inspired hundreds of thousands to be more personally effective, make more money, and have more fun in his workshops and presentations across the globe.

Roger is a master at teaching what works. He has delivered thousands of presentations for organizations like Northwestern Mutual, Harley-Davidson, the National Association of Realtors, and countless others. His audiences and his coaching clients all give rave reviews for the improvement they immediately see, both professionally and personally. Roger also spent eight years as a professional stand-up comic—so when he speaks, people laugh a ton and learn at the fastest rate possible.

Roger, his wife Shannon, and two sons reside in Madison, Wisconsin. He can be followed on Twitter @RogerSeip1, found on LinkedIn and Facebook, and checked out at www .deliverfreedom.com/bio_roger_seip.html.

## About Planet Freedom

**www.planetfreedom.com**
Learn. Discover. Grow. Be.

Throughout *Train Your Brain for Success*, you've been directed to www.planetfreedom.com. This is the home of Planet Freedom, a world where you can learn specific skills to optimize your life, discover what makes you tick, grow in ways you never thought possible, and be more of what you've always dreamed of being. It's also the place where you'll find all of your Memory Optimization™ exercises for these chapters and some great bonus materials to enhance your experience with this book. To access that support material, head to www.planetfreedom.com/trainyourbrain.

When you get there, you'll need an access code. If you're on a computer, use the access code **TYBFSBOOK**.

From your smartphone, you can simply scan this QR code:

Enjoy your experience there!

# Index